FORGIVENESS—GOD'S MASTER KEY

FORGIVENESS—GOD'S MASTER KEY

PETER HORROBIN

Sovereign World

Sovereign World Ltd
PO Box 784
Ellel
Lancaster LA1 9DA
England

www.sovereignworld.com
www.facebook.com/sovereignworld
www.twitter.com/sovereignworld

ISBN 978 1 85240 502 1

The publishers aim to produce books which will help to extend and build up the
Kingdom of God. We do not necessarily agree with every view expressed by the
authors, or with every interpretation of Scripture expressed. We expect readers to
make their own judgment in the light of their understanding of God's Word and in an
attitude of Christian love and fellowship.

Cover design by David Lund Design
Typeset by Hurix Systems Pvt. Limited

Contents

Jesus said,

*"Father, forgive them, for they do not
know what they are doing."*
Luke 23:34 *(NIV)*

Preface

God's Master Key is the most powerful prayer on Earth! Forgiveness is not only the key to the restoration of our relationship with God, but also the key to healing from the consequences of hurtful and damaging human relationships.

From the cross Jesus prayed those dramatic words to God, "Father, forgive them, for they do not know what they are doing." What an example He showed to us all about having a forgiving heart, even when people do dreadfully bad things.

Learning to pray this most powerful of prayers is the beginning of a lifetime's adventure with God. It will not only bring much healing to your past it will also open up new doors for you in the future. It is both God's Master Key and a key of miracles!

I know of many, many people whose lives have been totally transformed by God as they have lived out the consequences of praying this prayer. Some of their stories are in this book.

The first edition was simply called *The Most Powerful Prayer on Earth*. With added testimonies, from some of those who have put the forgiveness prayer into practice, the title of this new edition now reflects the fact that so many have found it to be the master key they had been looking for. A master key which unlocks the most difficult of problems.

I can guarantee that if you learn how to pray this prayer, sincerely from your heart, your life will never be the same again! You will be changed, your circumstances will also be changed and you, too, will have a story to tell of what God has done in your life.

Without forgiveness as a foundation stone of our faith, every time we are hurt by what someone else says or does, we will be encased in yet more bondage. Forgiveness is the master key that opens the door of hope and healing.

I pray you will want to walk with me in this exciting adventure of faith, use the master key and see what God does in your life as a result!

Peter Horrobin
September 2008

PART 1

FORGIVENESS—GOD'S MASTER KEY

Chapter 1

A Master Key

God's Way Out

A large house has many rooms and many doors. Each door has its own key. But a master key is designed to open any door in the building. The person with the master key can go anywhere.

The life we have each lived is like a building with many different rooms. Each room contains the memories of important events in life. Some of the doors are wide open all the time, and we happily enjoy the memories these rooms contain.

Other doors are closed, but we have no difficulty in opening them whenever we wish. There is no pain associated with the memories these rooms contain.

But some of the doors are both closed and locked. What lies behind these doors is too painful to look at, and often the key has been thrown away. Some of these rooms have names such as trauma, rejection, betrayal, abuse, disloyalty, divorce, accidents and many others.

People continue through life knowing there is unresolved pain lying behind these locked doors, caused by people who have really hurt them in the past. Sometimes also the pain is caused by their own mistakes, and they don't know how to resolve a situation for which they believe they are responsible. They do their very best to carry on regardless, but as the years go by it gets harder and harder to cover up the fact that they are hurting inside.

The homes of some people have so many locked doors that there is very little space left in which to live! They have closed the doors on the mess inside, hoping the doors will stay shut forever. Eventually, however, they cease to be able to function effectively as normal human beings. There can be so much hidden pain, trauma, anger, resentment or jealousy that they become less and less like the people God intended them to be.

Sometimes the mess on the inside seeps out from under the doors of the locked rooms. When it does, people try to cover it up and carry on as if nothing is happening. But everyone else can see the mess, and those we are in relationship with have to live with the consequences!

Sometimes people try to clean up the mess from the outside—but there always seems to be more mess coming from under the doors than they can cope with. They know that they can only deal with the problem properly by opening the door and going inside, but the key has been thrown away. They cannot open the doors by themselves. They need help. They need a new key.

Amazingly, Jesus left us a master key—a key so powerful and effective that it can open even the most stubborn of these locked doors. But He requires our cooperation to use it!

Jesus is not frightened of the mess that lies behind the doors. He wants to go in with us and help us clean it up. He personally designed this master key for you and for me. And then He showed us how to use it.

This golden master key is the most powerful prayer on Earth. It is totally life transforming! And right now, between the pages of this book, you are holding the instructions on how to use it.

No circumstance is so awful or devastating that it is beyond the relevance of this amazing prayer. Hannah was on a fast track to drugs and suicide. Her life had been ruined by years of cruel and painful sexual abuse in her family. She placed the master key in the door and prayed the prayer. God changed her life forever.

Michael was in despair because the wife he had loved so much had fallen for his best friend and walked out on him. When he prayed the prayer, his broken heart was healed, and he was able to start again and rebuild his life.

Lynda had lost hope. At twenty-six she was on a lifetime disability pension following a terrible accident. She prayed the prayer, and now she is married and living a normal life—no disability and no need for a pension.

Your circumstances might not be as bad as Hannah's, Michael's or Lynda's—or they might be worse! Whatever your circumstances are, when you learn to pray the most powerful prayer on Earth from your heart, things will change. They will change because you, who have always been part of your circumstances, will also be changed!

Read on and learn how to use this wonderful life-transforming master key.

Chapter 2

The Most Powerful
Prayer on Earth
Spiritual Dynamite

Jesus not only taught us how to pray, but He also taught us
how to use spiritual dynamite! Toward the end of His life He
found Himself in an impossible situation. There was no way
out. What was He going to do?

The Prayer That Jesus Prayed

After three wonderful years of teaching and healing people,
the tables were turned against Jesus. He was now facing
crucifixion (see Luke 23). Many different people had played
a part in the unfolding scenario that led to His present situation.

First, there were the religious leaders. They were jealous of
Jesus' popularity and threatened by His power and authority.
They hated Him.

Next, there was Judas—the sadly deluded disciple who
thought that thirty pieces of silver was a fair price for betray-
ing his master. He eventually committed suicide.

trial there was Pilate, the weak-willed governor of an province of Judea, who tried to wash his hands of responsibility for what was happening.

And then there was Herod, the powerless Jewish king, to whom Pilate sent Jesus for a second opinion but who only ridiculed and mocked Him! The chief priests and the teachers of the law watched the performance and vehemently accused Him.

In Jerusalem for the Passover Feast was a large crowd of visitors. Urged on by the authorities, they were incited to clamor for Jesus' execution. They insistently demanded, "Crucify Him! Crucify Him!"

And let's not forget Barabbas, the notorious criminal who gained his freedom at the expense of Jesus' life.

At Jesus' arrest and crucifixion there were the Roman soldiers. They were simply obeying the orders of their commanding officer as they drove the nails through Jesus' body and into the cross. They cast lots for His clothes and mocked Him with cruel words, "If you are the king of the Jews, save yourself."

And finally there were you and I, alongside every other human being there has ever been.

All of these people, including you and me, were responsible for Jesus' being led out to Calvary to be crucified. He met His death alongside two common criminals who were also scheduled for execution on the same day.

In the beginning, humankind turned its back on the God who made it and broke relationship with Him. As a result, death entered into the human race. It was our sin, therefore, that caused the Father to put the only possible rescue plan into effect that could restore the broken relationship between God and humankind. God loved the world so much that He gave His only Son to pay the ultimate price for sin on our behalf—when Jesus died on the cross. *Our sin took Jesus there. Jesus' love kept Him there!*

There is no one else who has ever walked the face of this earth, either before or since, who suffered such terrible injustice. No one else has ever had a greater excuse to blame others and cry out, "Not fair."

So what did Jesus do? He prayed, and this is what He prayed: "Father, forgive them, for they do not know what they are doing." *I believe this is the single most powerful prayer that has ever been prayed!* Not only did Jesus walk in personal forgiveness toward all of those who were the agents of His suffering, but He also asked God to forgive them.

To ask God to forgive, in circumstances such as these, was an extraordinary demonstration of what Jesus meant when He said, "Bless those who curse you, pray for those who mistreat you" (Luke 6:28, *NASB*). Jesus was asking His Father to allow those who had persecuted Him to enter into the wonderful benefits that He had planned and purposed for them, benefits such as joy, release from bondage and, the greatest of all, a relationship with Himself.

All the angels of heaven must have bowed in silent wonder as they saw their beloved Jesus turn His back on resentment, bitterness, anger and revenge as He asked the Father to forgive all those would contribute to His death. What a man! What a God!

The Need for a Forgiving Heart

It is impossible to ask God to forgive those who have hurt us without first forgiving them from the heart ourselves. Jesus even said that if we do not forgive those who have hurt us, then our Father in heaven will not forgive us (see Matt. 6:15)!

People are often surprised to find that this is in the Bible. Surely God wants to forgive us, they say. Yes, He does, but He has also given us a choice; and He won't override the choices we make. *If we choose not to forgive those who have hurt us, we put ourselves under their control. If we are under their control, we cannot be free for God to heal us and set us free.* If Jesus had not forgiven all those who had hurt Him, it would have changed His relationship with Father God.

When we confess our own sin to God but refuse to forgive others, we are asking God to do something for us that we are not willing to do for others. That's hypocrisy.

Jesus told a parable about a servant who was forgiven a massive debt of millions of dollars by the king but who refused to write off a tiny debt of a few dollars from his neighbor. The king threw the servant into prison until he could repay the entire amount! Jesus warned that those who behave like the servant will never know freedom (see Matt. 18:21-35).

Jesus even told us to love our enemies! He knew that if we reacted in bitterness of heart against those who oppose us and who even do bad things to us, we would be in bondage to those people for as long as we live. He knew that if we ignore this vital principle, we will find that our reaction to what others have done to us could do us as much harm as the original offense. He wanted us to be free from all that.

Only when we have truly forgiven others will we be able to pray Jesus' prayer "Father, forgive them" from the heart. *Forgiveness of others is the huge first step that leads to our total release from the chains surrounding a hurting heart.*

Change from the Inside Out

I was teaching at a conference in Hungary just as the Communist walls in Russia and Eastern Europe were falling down. The last Russian tanks were leaving Budapest. The people who had come to the conference were from the surrounding Communist-controlled nations.

As I looked at this large body of severely oppressed Christians, my heart went out to them in their need. I felt a portion of the grief that God must have felt at all they had suffered. Many were suffering physically, and their physical disposition reflected their internal pain.

I took a huge risk and talked to them about forgiving their Communist oppressors. I didn't know how they would respond, but the Spirit of God was changing them on the inside as they began to understand what Jesus said about forgiving even our enemies.

One by one people began to stand up as they made the choice to forgive. Then suddenly they were all standing as the truth of God's Word sank in. Through the translator, I led them in a prayer, and phrase by phrase they spoke out their forgiveness.

The Spirit of God fell upon the people—in the very hall where, in past years, Communist leaders had met for their conferences! I spoke out, as the Scriptures say, that Jesus had come to set the captives free, and then I took authority over the powers of darkness that were holding these people in bondage.

Healing began to flow from Father God into His hurting people. They were changing on the inside, and very soon their bodies began to reflect the deep inner healing they were experiencing.

Never in all my years of ministering healing to people around the world have I seen God do so much healing among so many people in such a short space of time! People were literally walking taller as, through forgiveness, the spiritual oppression over them was broken and bent and hurting backs were restored.

I watched a miracle take place before my very eyes. As the people forgave their oppressors, they experienced first hand the wonderful power of God that is liberated through the simple act of forgiveness from the heart.

The Power of the Prayer

"Father, forgive them" is the most powerful prayer that you can ever pray.

- It transforms your relationship with God.
- It releases the power of the Holy Spirit into your life.
- It restores your soul.
- It opens the door to God's healing.
- It transforms your relationships with other people.

But none of us can truly pray this extraordinary prayer until we have learned to forgive others for what they have done to us. And sometimes we need to forgive ourselves before we are able to turn our hearts toward blessing other people.

Stephen, the first Christian martyr, learned the lesson of forgiveness well. He had such a forgiving attitude toward his accusers that when he was stoned to death—with the man who became the apostle Paul watching on—he, too, was able to pray the most powerful prayer on Earth. With words very similar to those Jesus had used, he prayed, "Lord, do not hold this sin against them" (Acts 7:60).

How important it is that we learn to live like this in the ordinary circumstances of life and not just when facing the extremes of persecution that Stephen and countless others have faced through the centuries!

Learning to pray this amazing prayer from your heart could be the most important thing you will ever do. It is God's master key, specially designed to unlock the most stubborn of problems in your life.

It is the spiritual dynamite that God uses to blow apart the prison doors—those doors that can keep us locked into the pain of the past. It is the most powerful prayer on Earth.

Chapter 3

Forgive and Be Forgiven

God's Divine Law of Blessing

Every day people exceed the speed limit in their cars. They break the law of the land in which they live. But unless they are caught in a speed trap, nothing happens. Laws such as this are man-made, and men are needed to enforce them.

The Laws of the Universe

There are other laws in the universe, however, that are not man-made, and if we ignore them, there are consequences, even if there is no one there to enforce them. These laws are both physical and spiritual!

Take, for example, the law of gravity. If you drop a coin, it falls to the floor. If you step off a cliff, your body will obey the law of gravity and you will fall downward, probably to your death. Everything in the universe obeys the law of gravity. No one can ignore it—not even for a moment. Nothing and no one can ever change it.

There are many other physical laws that control the whole of the physical universe. All of them are unchangeable. They are a reflection both of the unchangeable character of creator God and of the order He built into the universe.

The early pioneers of science focused their attentions on discovering these laws. Without such laws and the order that they bring, the physical universe would be nothing but chaos. Life would be impossible and human beings could not survive.

Men and women are physical beings and are subject to these physical laws. But there is more to a human being, however, than just having a physical body. Humans are also spiritual beings. Not only are the shape and design of the human body unique, but the human character and personality also are totally unique. In many different places the Bible uses words such as "soul" and "spirit" to describe this spiritual nature (see Pss. 35:9; 51:10; 1Thess. 5:23; Heb. 4:12).

So we are both physical and spiritual beings. Because we are physical, we are subject to the laws of the physical universe. But because we are spiritual, we are also subject to the spiritual laws that God has built into the spiritual universe.

And because we live at the interface between the physical and spiritual worlds, what happens in the physical can affect the spiritual and what happens in the spiritual can also affect the physical.

As children we quickly learn about the dangers of ignoring physical laws. Our parents try to protect us from discovering the law of gravity by protecting us from falling down stairs and the laws of motion by keeping us away from dangerous traffic.

But where do we learn about the dangers of ignoring spiritual laws?

It was God's intention that our parents should not only teach us vital physical lessons but also teach us equally vital spiritual lessons. For just as there can be very serious physical consequences of being ignorant of the physical laws, there can be consequences even more serious of being ignorant of the spiritual laws. Ignoring physical laws has a serious consequence in time, but ignoring spiritual laws can have a serious consequence in eternity as well!

Because you and I—and all humankind—chose to rebel against the God who made us, relationship with Him was broken. As a result we lost the understanding of these spiritual principles, which we would otherwise have understood naturally.

But God loved us so much that He did two things to help us: First, He gave us His written Word (the Bible) so that we could understand about spiritual things and learn what the consequences are of ignoring spiritual laws. Then He sent His Son, Jesus (the living Word), so that we could have a restored relationship with Him.

Jesus tells us that one of the reasons He came was to show us what Father God is really like, for He and the Father are one. He told His disciples that if they had seen Him, they had also seen the Father (see John 14:7-9).

The Law of Forgiveness

Every one of us has free will—the ability to make choices about anything and everything in life. We can make right choices or wrong choices, good choices or bad choices. The right and good choices will bring blessing into our lives. The wrong and bad choices will have the opposite effect.

And this brings us right back to the most powerful prayer on Earth! To pray this amazing prayer it is necessary to embrace a principle that is right at the heart of God's spiritual laws. Make the right choice concerning this principle and you are headed for blessing!

The disciples were asking Jesus how to pray. Jesus' answer was to give them a pattern that would form the basis of all our prayers. We call it the Lord's Prayer (see Matt. 6:9-13; Luke 11:1-4).

All who believe in God and pray want to know that their sins are forgiven. They don't want their unforgiven sins to remain on God's slate for eternity and be a barrier between them and God. Therefore, it would have been a relief to the disciples to hear Jesus include within the Lord's Prayer a phrase that began, "Forgive us our trespasses" (see Matt. 6:12).

We trespass when we go beyond what we are allowed. If we ignore the "Private" signs and walk on someone else's land, we are trespassing. When we step over God's line, the line that divides what is right from what is wrong, we are trespassing against God. We leave behind our spiritual footprints—God knows where we have been!

Just as human relationships are damaged when we trespass on someone else's property, relationships with God are damaged when we trespass spiritually. Our conscience is affected and we know we have done wrong.

Deep inside we long for restoration of relationship. To deal with the situation we need to face up to our pride and humbly come back to God. We need to say we are sorry and ask for forgiveness for our sin. Humility is the gateway to God's grace!

The Lord's Prayer brings us to this point of asking God for forgiveness, but then we suddenly find that the next phrase contains some unwelcome and challenging words! Not only does it say, "Forgive us our trespasses," but it also says, "as we forgive those who trespass against us." It is here that we come up against one of those vital spiritual laws—laws that cannot be changed and laws that we are subject to even though we don't want to be, whether we like it or not!

The disciples must have struggled with the idea of having to forgive others as well, for Jesus had to tell them again—and in very simple words: "If you don't forgive others for what they have done to you, neither will my Father in Heaven forgive you" (see Matt. 6:15).

Peter, one of Jesus' disciples, even asked Jesus how often he needed to forgive others, suggesting that perhaps seven was a very large and generous number! There was a gentle rebuke in Jesus' words when He replied, "Not seven times, Peter, but seventy times seven" (see Matt. 18:21-22). In other words, stop counting and just keep on forgiving!

The Law of Blessing

If we want to know the continuous blessing of God, then we have to be continuously forgiving of other people. Otherwise when we ask God to forgive us, we will be asking Him for something that we are not willing to give to others. We will become trapped by our own hypocrisy.

There is no way that Jesus could have prayed the most powerful prayer on Earth if He had not first come to the point of forgiving those who were nailing Him to that piece of wood. He knew that forgiveness of others was an essential gateway to knowing the continuous blessing of God. This is what He had taught His disciples to do time and time again.

Forgiveness of sin is the greatest possible blessing that God makes available to His children, but if we are not willing to forgive others, we will miss out on God's best for our lives.

Consider the examples of Mary and Alec, who discovered the blessing that comes with forgiveness. Mary had been sexually abused by her father for many years, and she also had done many wrong things, including having several wrong sexual relationships. In the arms of other men, she was looking for the comfort her father should have given her.

Mary knew these relationships had been wrong and she confessed them to God with many tears. She knew she had done the right thing in confessing them, but she didn't feel much different as a result, and she couldn't understand why.

It was then that she had to face the hardest decision of her life—whether or not she would choose to forgive her own father. How could she, after he had done such terrible things to her? But deep inside she knew that it was her attitude towards her father that was a barrier preventing her from knowing the forgiveness of God for herself.

Mary slowly faced the issue, and she realized that if she didn't forgive her father, the thoughts of what he had done would control her for the rest of her life. She wanted to be free so very much, and yet to be so, she had to give up all the bitterness and anger in her heart.

Finally the battle was won and she was able to forgive him. It was only then that she also knew the full depth of God's love for her as He lifted the burden of her own sins. She experienced the blessing of God in a totally new way—just as Jesus had said in Matthew 6:14.

Mary had learned that we can't ignore God's spiritual law of forgiveness. It is just as powerful in the spiritual realms as is the law of gravity in the physical realms. Ignore the law and we bring suffering on ourselves; abide by the law and we walk in God's blessing.

Alec struggled desperately with what he thought was the unfairness of having to forgive others—until he had experienced in his heart the joy and blessing of forgiving the person who had hurt him the most. He was then a totally different man, desperate to think of anyone else he could forgive so that he could enjoy more of the blessing!

Mary and Alec, and thousands like them, discovered God's spiritual laws the hard way. By ignoring the command of God to forgive, they discovered the law that bound them in spiritual chains. When they forgave, they discovered another law—this time a law of blessing. Then they began to know the forgiveness of God for themselves. They learned the relationship between forgiving others and being forgiven, and they began to taste for themselves the blessings God promises.

Chapter 4

But They Don't Deserve It!
The Biggest Obstacle

True! When people do bad things that hurt others they don't deserve to be forgiven. Jesus could have taken this line with everyone involved in the events that led up to Calvary, from the crowds who shouted "Crucify him!" to the soldiers who drove the nails through His hands. And He would have been right, they didn't deserve to be forgiven!

But instead He cried out to God, saying, "Father, forgive them! They don't know what they are doing!"

Forgiveness doesn't seem to make any sense—and it especially doesn't make sense to think this way when we are hurting so very deeply because of what others have done to us. A sense of injustice rises up from within and shouts out, "It's not fair!"

Forgiveness doesn't make sense—until we understand that forgiveness is always an act of love and never an act of justice. It's important that we understand the difference between forgiveness and justice.

The Demand for Justice

When a man is arrested for stealing, justice requires that he pay for the crime by returning what has been stolen to its rightful owner, by spending time in jail or paying a fine. The Bible makes this point very clearly when it describes some of the punishments that were appropriate for particular crimes—justice had to be done.

When the debt to society has been paid a former criminal is said to be a free man. But is he? Well, that depends on how we look at things. As far as society is concerned, the man is free again to go about his legitimate affairs. As long as his behavior remains within the law he will remain a free man for the rest of his days. But is he really free?

Real freedom for the criminal can only come when he also says sorry for what he has done to the person he has wronged, receives forgiveness and, where possible, does everything he can to make restitution for his crime.

This, however, only deals with the human consequences of the man's sin. In reality, not only has he done wrong against the victim of his crime and society, but he has also broken one of God's commandments and come up against one of God's spiritual laws. He can make it right with society and the person he has stolen from, but can he ever make it right with God?

We have already established that humans are both physical and spiritual beings and that there are spiritual consequences of the physical things we do. When we do wrong our relationship with God is damaged and we wrap ourselves in spiritual chains as a result. No one needs to put us in a spiritual prison for what we have done, we are already there!

It's a bit like gravity! In the physical realm, once we step off the edge of a cliff we don't have any choice about whether we fall or not. We will fall downwards whether we like it or not.

In exactly the same way, when we choose to rebel against the God who made us and we ignore the spiritual laws that He has built into the spiritual universe, we will fall into a prison created by our own choices.

Once we have stepped off the spiritual cliff, it's too late. We find ourselves in a prison from which there is no obvious way out. Just as human justice requires that the price of crime must be paid, eternal justice requires that the price of sin also be paid.

But if, for example, you have been put in a physical prison because you cannot pay the fine that has been demanded by the judge, there is no way that you can get out and earn the money to pay the fine. You are in an impossible situation. You don't have the money in prison to pay the fine and you can't get out of prison to earn money until the fine has been paid! It requires someone who is not in prison to come and pay the fine.

The problem with sin is that every human being who has ever walked the face of this earth is in the same prison! We have all walked off the edge of the same spiritual cliff and discovered that spiritual gravity is as unchangeable as physical gravity!

Our relationship with God has been broken and we are all in jail. And what is more, there is no other human being out there who is able to pay the fine and meet the requirements of justice. We are all trapped in the same prison except, that is, for Jesus—the one human being who never sinned and could never, therefore, have had a reason for being put in jail!

Jesus was the totally sinless Son of God who came to Earth as a human being. Oh, yes, He was tempted often enough, but He never sinned. Jesus never allowed Himself to come under the control of others. He never stepped off the edge of a spiritual cliff to discover the consequences of spiritual

gravity! And He always made the right choices, never end-
ing up in the spiritual prison that has entrapped every other
human being.

As a sinless human being Jesus was in a position to plead
the case of sinners and pay the price for those in jail. The
ultimate price for sin is a broken relationship with the God
who made us—or, putting it another way, death!

Because Jesus had never sinned, He was not in prison with
us, so when He paid the price of our sin through dying on
the cross, there was no crime attached to His record and the
jailer could not keep Him in prison. Even death could not
control Him (see Acts 2:24)!

It was as if He went to prison on our behalf or paid the fine
that we each deserved to pay. Justice was done. He became
united to the whole of the human race through His death.
He knew what it was like to feel forsaken by God the Father.
But because He was otherwise a free man, death could not
keep Him bound. The resurrection was a certain next step—
it was a matter of when it would happen, not if!

Through the death of Jesus, then, the price for sin was
paid and justice was done. God made a way for the spiritual
(eternal) consequences of human sin to be dealt with.

Peace with God

Unconfessed and unforgiven sin has a habit of working away
at us on the inside. What began as a spiritual problem can,
in time, become a physical problem. When Jesus healed a
paralyzed man, He first dealt with forgiveness of the man's
sins. James tells us that we need to confess our sins one to
another so that we will be healed (see James 5:16).

The story of Tania illustrates the peace that confession
brings. At the end of a conference session that I was teaching about healing, Tania came up to me and confessed that

she had been embezzling money from her employer and now owed him thousands of dollars. The knowledge of what she had done was crippling her on the inside. The stolen money had not brought her the pleasure she had anticipated.

As she poured out her confession to God, she knew that her only way forward was to confess her sin to her employer and make restitution. She went away that night full of apprehension about what was going to happen in the office the next day, but she also went away at peace with God for the first time since she had started stealing the money. Her healing had begun.

Returning now to our criminal who had been arrested for stealing, once he deals with the human consequences of his crime, what should he do in order to be totally free? All that remains is that he trust Jesus as his Saviour and ask God to forgive him, as an act of love, for his sins.

None of us deserves such generous treatment. We don't deserve to be forgiven for anything we have done—it was only made possible because God is a God of love and because His Son, Jesus, willingly paid the price, ensuring that in the courts of heaven justice had been done.

It is certainly true that our criminal does not deserve to be forgiven, but the sad fact is that neither do you nor I. Ultimately, we are all guilty of the same crime—rebellion against a holy God—and we have all landed in the same jail! Or to use a different analogy, we are all in the same boat. Yes, some people may do things that are much worse than others, but the spiritual and eternal consequences are just the same.

The Freedom of Forgiveness

A similar principle operates with respect to forgiveness. Irrespective of whether what has been done to you is large or small, the end-result of unforgiveness is the same. When we choose not to forgive someone bitterness, resentment and anger build up and then take root inside us. They act like cancers on our emotions and we get all knotted up inside—no matter how much in the right we may think we are and how much in the wrong the other person may have been.

We can make comparisons between us and them, elevate ourselves to a place of superiority and justify our lack of forgiveness to others on the grounds that we are much better than they are, but in reality it doesn't help us at all.

It may be true that the people who have really hurt us have sinned against us to a much greater degree than we could ever have done to them. But that doesn't minimise the effect it is having on us on the inside!

The offence we have already suffered is added to day by day as a result of our own unforgiveness. Finally it becomes all consuming; and the very person we are becomes lost in a sea of resentment, which can lead to years of emotional, psychological and even physical conditions (see Heb. 12:15).

If you want to be free of the poison of bitterness, and healed of the devastating consequences unforgiveness can have on your health, your family and all your relationships, then you need to make a choice to start forgiving now. Only then will you be able to follow Jesus' example and pray the most powerful prayer on Earth, "Father, forgive them."

When you have reached the place of being able to ask God to forgive those who have hurt you, the chains of bondage will begin to fall away and you will be able at last to walk free.

Jenny's story illustrates the freedom that forgiveness brings; Jenny had suffered unspeakable things at the hands of her mother. Thirty years later Jenny's life was only sustainable through high doses of medication from her psychiatrist. Her whole life was in the balance. Suicide seemed an attractive way out.

In reality, although she had had no relationship with her mother for many years, her mother still controlled her from the inside. The chains of unforgiveness kept all the memories and suffering of childhood fresh in her mind. She was totally trapped.

Forgiving her mother seemed like the most dangerous and unfair walk Jenny could ever go on. It felt like an impossible journey. But little by little Jenny took the steps and walked away from the pain of the past.

The chains of bondage were broken and now Jenny is free to be herself for the first time in her life. Forgiving her mother began the process of personal healing from the pain of the past; praying that God would bless her mother meant that Jenny would stay free in the future!

Jenny's mother didn't deserve to be forgiven, but not forgiving her was condemning Jenny to hell on earth! *Learning to pray the most powerful prayer on Earth set Jenny free for ever!*

Chapter 5

Starting with Parents

*The Importance of Forgiving Our
Parents for Everything*

Whether you like it or not, your parents are still the most important people in your life! They contributed more to who and what you are than anyone else on the planet. And that's the case even if you were given away by your parents on the day you were born and you have never seen either of them since!

Contrary to what those who promote abortion as a woman's right tell us about aborted babies, you were a human being from the moment of your conception. For that reason even the circumstances of that most momentous occasion of your life could even be having an effect on you now.

On the one hand this very earliest of influences from your parents could have provided you with the most wonderful of starts to life, surrounded by loving care and tenderness. On the other hand it could have been the most horrific of traumatic experiences as your mother was violently raped by an intruder. Most people began life somewhere in between these two extremes.

Facing Our Inheritance

Even if you had the most loving of starts to life and were a much wanted baby, your parents nevertheless were a long way from being perfect. They inherited the consequences of their own parents' inadequacies and upbringing, and their parents inherited from the previous generation and so on. All of us are the fruit of our ancestors, and not everything we have inherited from them is good.

This may sound like bad news! And you may well be asking, "What's the point of telling me all this when there is absolutely nothing I can do to change what happened in the past?"

I agree that if there were nothing at all you could do, it would simply be an act of cruelty to remind people of irresolvable problems from their past! All it would do is create unnecessary anger and make whatever problems a person has seem even worse!

It is absolutely true that you cannot change the influence that your great-grandparents had on your grandparents and the influence your grandparents had on your parents. It is also true that you cannot now go back in time and change the circumstances of your own conception.

Neither can you change anything that happened during those vital nine months in your mother's womb or what happened during the most dangerous journey of your life from the security of the womb into the arms of the midwife or doctor on the day you were born.

Your early childhood and nurturing also were outside your control. All you could do was receive what was offered, be it good or bad. Whatever early schooling you had was not your choice. All your early education was organized by others, and you had to either enjoy or endure the schooling your parents provided for you.

In fact it probably wasn't until your teenage years that you began to make your own choices about the things that have really mattered to you in life. But by the time you got to the place of making responsible adult decisions, you may already have been messed up as a result of the weaknesses and wrong choices of your own parents, about which you had no option.

So when your turn came to make choices for yourself, guess what. You began to repeat the same sort of mistakes they did and, what's worse, probably made some new ones of your own. These new mistakes add to the burden you pass on to your own children!

"What a mess," I hear you saying. I agree! So what's the point of even knowing all this? The point is this: *You cannot change anything of the inheritance your parents have left you. But God can change you right now, if you give Him a chance, so that you don't have to continue to suffer the ongoing consequences.*

Cutting the Chains

In the first chapter we talked about there being many different rooms in the house of your life. For most people the bad memories of parental problems are well and truly placed behind closed doors. They have been locked away—hopefully, they think, forever.

People then try to make the best of what life has offered them, without thinking that there is a master key to all those rooms and that God can clean up the mess that's on the other side of the doors.

No, God can't change the facts of what has happened in the past, but He can change you in the present so that you need not have to endure the consequences of these things for the rest of your days.

And you've guessed right, the master key to it all is forgiveness. Without using this key those doors will never be opened. And unless those rooms are cleaned out, the poison that lies behind the locked doors will never stop seeping out into the remainder of your life.

By using the key of forgiveness you can walk away from the past and with God's help start again. Whatever legacy your parents have left you, they really didn't know what the consequences could be of their own mistakes. It was impossible for them to comprehend that what they were doing could cause you such problems now.

The Bible puts it this way: "Our ancestors sinned, but now they are gone, and we are suffering for their sins" (Lam. 5:7, *TEV*). This reality also is clearly expressed within the Ten Commandments (see Exod. 20:5). This seems very unfair until we realize that God's original intention was that children would be influenced for good by the good things that come down to them from their parents, grandparents and even great-grandparents (see Exod. 20:6). But just as a rainwater pipe is able to carry clean or dirty water equally effectively, because of the Fall, the channel that God created to bless can equally be used to carry the consequences of the sins of humankind down the family line as well as blessings.

We need to thank God for all the good things that have come to us from our parents and ancestors and begin the work of forgiving them for everything that's come to us that has acted as a curse on our lives. As we do this it's as if chains that are holding us in bondage to the past are cut, beginning the work of freeing us to become the people God intended us to be.

Setting Ourselves Free

In the children's story *Gulliver's Travels*, Jonathan Swift tells us how Gulliver ends up in Lilliput, the country of tiny people. The people there find this "giant" fast asleep and wonder how they can protect themselves from him when he wakes up.

What they did was to tie him down with thousands of strands of what were to Gulliver fine cotton, though to the Lilliputians they were rope. For Gulliver any one of those strands could have been snapped in a fraction of a second with the minimum of effort; but because there were so many of them, he was held tight and when he woke up, he was unable to move!

Most of the things from the past that hold us down are like strands of fine cotton. Though each one has little power on its own, often there are so many that together they cripple us.

The most powerful prayer on Earth simply asks us to say, "Father, forgive them. They didn't know what they were doing." For some people this is an easy prayer to pray in respect to our parents and ancestors. We can easily understand that since they couldn't have known of our existence, how could they possibly have known what effect their behavior was going to have on us?

For other people this is a really hard prayer. Because they see so many problems that have come to them from their parents, they have become very angry men or women. Bitterness has taken root inside them, and the last thing they want to do is to forgive the people who have caused them such pain and heartache all their lives.

Consider the story of one lady who was struggling with rapidly developing arthritis in her joints. She could no longer dance and enjoy life. Her mother had also been a severe arthritic before she died. As the woman spoke out forgiveness to her parents and to everyone in her family line who had done things that had hurt her, God began to change her from the inside out.

It wasn't long before the pain and the arthritis in her joints had disappeared and she was able to dance again. It was only a small step that she took—to pray, "Father, forgive them"—but that step took her a giant leap forward in both understanding and healing.

Why don't you spend a little while thinking about your parents and thanking God for all the good things that came to you through them? Then you can begin to forgive them and all your ancestors before them for everything they've said or done that has had a negative effect on your life.

It may take quite a long time to work through all your feelings, but every time you forgive someone for something new you find, one of the strands that is holding you prisoner is being cut. Little by little you are setting yourself free from the chains of your past.

As you pray the most powerful prayer on Earth, God is able to put new strength back into your life and take you a step nearer to fulfilling the destiny He has for you.

Chapter 6

⟨⟩⟩

Dealing with Thieves and Robbers

*Freedom from Those Who Have Stolen
Part of Our Lives*

Losses occur when thieves and robbers steal things that don't belong to them. When ordinary things of life such as cash, a camera or a computer are stolen from us, we lose the monetary value of those items.

In addition to this monetary value, we also lose the special added value attached to certain items of great personal significance for us or our family—items such as a family heirloom, photographs, a much-loved car, a favorite piece of jewelry or something very personal that could have little or no monetary value but to us is utterly precious.

Such losses can be a very powerful source of personal pain; and if they are not dealt with by forgiving the offenders and praying the most powerful prayer on Earth, we will always end up in bitterness, anger and even fear of what else people might take.

When something is stolen from us, it is as if there is a strand of invisible rope stretching out from us to the thief. It is unforgiveness that holds each strand of the rope in place. Unforgiveness is like spiritual superglue—it acts instantly and sticks forever!

We could easily shake off the limiting effect of one such strand; but when there are many strands, they join together to make a rope that limits us because it can influence, and even control, every aspect of life. And every time we think about the person who has done these things to us and we reinforce our feelings of bitterness and resentment through further expressions of unforgiveness, we strengthen the rope and add more superglue to its fixing!

This process can even be passed down the generational line, with one generation after another nursing a grudge of hatred and unforgiveness against the culprits and their descendants. For example, even today, there are MacDonalds who only very reluctantly would have anything to do with a Campbell because of what the Campbells did several hundred years ago in the terrible massacre of Glencoe!

The more we find security in our possessions, the more difficult it is to forgive those who have taken precious things from us. But in reality there are much more important things in life than our possessions, and we need to get to a place in our relationship with God where our ultimate security is in Him, not in the property we own.

I've Been Robbed!

However important our possessions may be to us and however hard it may be to forgive someone who has robbed us of them, the effect of the loss is nowhere near as great as the loss caused by a completely different kind of theft! Most possessions can be replaced, often very quickly, but the things I am talking about now can never be replaced; the effects of their loss can only be healed.

What I am referring to are things like character, reputation, identity, sexuality, time, and even health, children and family. We will look at just four of these as examples of the many ways you could be robbed of significant things in your life—your character, your sexuality, your time and your health.

The pain of having these things stolen from us is far greater and more consequential than the loss of any mere possessions, but the remedy for being healed is exactly the same as for the theft of our possessions—the most powerful prayer on Earth!

Reputation

Unkind and untrue words spoken about us by others have a habit of being passed around as gossip. By the time the stories have gone their rounds and sometimes been added to by people in the chain, everyone who has heard and believed them has lowered their opinion of us. Something of our reputation has been stolen.

When people put such words in print or perhaps release them on the Internet, the effect is even more serious, for they are now in a permanent format and can be read for as long as copies of the words are available.

Many years ago certain people said and wrote totally untrue words about me and the ministry I am involved in. Even today I come across people whose first instinct is to have nothing to do with us because of the words that were lodged in their memories.

The laws of most countries have provisions to protect the good name of individuals from such slander and libel. Not only is it a serious legal offense to steal a man's good name, but also it is a very serious offense before God (see Exod. 20:16; Prov. 19:5; Matt. 15:19-20).

However, the fact that what they were doing is wrong does not give me an excuse to harbor bitterness against such thieves in my own heart! By doing so I would only make it harder for people to find out the truth and change their opinion. Each time I come across someone who has been negatively affected by the words people have said or written is a fresh opportunity to forgive them and pray the most powerful prayer on Earth! Ultimately truth will be revealed, and God has to be the vindicator of our reputation.

Jesus suffered in this way, so we should not be surprised if it happens to us. How can it be that someone who did so much good, healed so many people and taught so many wonderful truths could become the victim of so many false accusations from false witnesses and a baying crowd that cried out to the authorities for His blood?

People stole His reputation. They had done Him a terrible disservice. But "Father, forgive them" was ultimately all that Jesus said. He could only have prayed this prayer to God if His own heart was forgiving towards those who had hurt Him.

Jesus was given a marvelous opportunity to defend His own reputation when Pilate, the Roman governor, asked Him to explain who He was. But Jesus chose not to answer the question and stood in silence before Pilate (see John 19:6-12).

Jesus may have been crucified on the strength of the false accusations of His accusers, but three days later it was God Himself who vindicated Him! Everything they had said about Jesus was demonstrated to be untrue on Resurrection morning!

The only way to deal with those who try to steal your character and your reputation is to forgive them, keep on doing what is right, act with humility and integrity, and trust God with the outcome.

In this way, as you forgive those who speak or write wrong things about you, the spiritual superglue of unforgiveness will never get a chance to attach the ropes of bitterness to your heart.

Sometimes even the opinions of your friends may be lowered because of what others say about you. That hurts, but you will suffer even more if you remain unforgiving in your heart. And this can even have an effect on your health and your ability to function in the way God intended.

Sexuality

Abuse comes in many forms—physical abuse, psychological abuse—but the form that has been exposed as being of epidemic proportions in today's world is sexual abuse.

Sexual abuse occurs when a sexual predator takes advantage of another human being in order to satisfy his or her perverted sexual desires and urges. This form of abuse can range from the visual voyeurism of a peeping Tom at one end of the scale to unwelcome sexual touching, sexual violence and rape or ritualistic sex at the other end of the scale. When it is all over, the abuser moves on to the next challenge without giving thought to the damage that has been done to the victim.

Men and women, boys and girls—all can be sexually abused; and the abuse can be heterosexual or homosexual in nature. Whenever one person is unwillingly forced into some aspect of sexual activity against his or her will, abuse has taken place.

Sexuality is a wonderful gift from God, which He intended to be enjoyed and completed within the safe confines of an intimate marital relationship. Anything that deprives a person of his or her free will in the area of sexuality is a serious form of theft. When a woman is abused or raped, she is robbed of the intimate joy of giving herself freely to her husband—and to her husband alone. Each time abuse takes place something more of the person is stolen.

God's plan for marriage is that both parties to the relationship would give something of themselves to the other.

A beautiful and godly relationship is established through this God-ordained tie. However, when a person is forced to give himself or herself sexually, the tie between them is very ungodly.

Only God can undo an ungodly tie and unscramble the mess. I have seen extraordinary healings take place in every culture of the world as people have brought the pain of such abuse to the light, forgave the abusers and prayed the most powerful prayer on Earth.

Forgiveness is the miracle key that allows God to undo the ties of abusive relationships and begin the work of healing and restoration. The past can't be undone, but the future can be different as God heals the broken heart.

Time

Each of us only has one life to live, and every available minute is a gift from God. Every minute matters and we all get justifiably upset when someone robs us of time. But how would you react if someone placed you in prison unfairly—for a crime you did not commit—and then left you there for a generation?

Nelson Mandela spent close to thirty years in prison at the hands of the ruling white authorities in the Republic of South Africa. His crime? Opposing the cruel and abusive apartheid regime that robbed the black communities of their right to land, resources and dignity as human beings.

He was robbed of a huge portion of his life. Few people have been robbed of so much time and kept such a forgiving heart as he did toward those who had imprisoned him for alleged political offenses. He was eventually released and vindicated, becoming the first democratically elected president of South Africa!

In the latter stages of his life he became an elder statesman on the world stage, having regained far more stature than he could possibly have dreamed of during his years in prison. How did this happen? He turned the master key in the lock of personal bondage and lived out consequences of praying the most powerful prayer on Earth.

The chains of hatred were cut and he walked free from his physical jail on Robben Island. Not only did he walk free from Robben Island, but he also walked free from being isolated on an island of bitterness for the rest of his days.

Health

Health and strength are prerequisites for the maximum enjoyment of all that life has to offer. But how do you cope when you are suddenly trapped in a damaged body as the result of a terrible accident that wasn't your fault? The sense of loss and the pain of injustice are totally understandable and normal feelings.

I briefly mentioned Lynda in chapter 1. Let me tell you more of her story: At the age of twenty-three, Lynda was on a night hike with other young people from her church when she fell off a cliff into a ravine. She lay there for over ten hours, with her back fractured in four places, before she was air-lifted out by helicopter.

Three years later, disabled and on a pension for life, suffering constant pain and chronic fatigue, she was without hope of fulfilling any of her dreams. Career, marriage and all the fun of life lay devastated at the place where she fell.

She never should have fallen off that cliff. The leader of the hike had split off from the group, leaving the group on a path headed for the edge of a cliff. Even though it was night, the leader failed to warn the rest of the danger. As Lynda tried to follow those ahead of her, she slipped off the cliff edge and fell into open space.

When we began to pray for her, there were many things that God did to bring about her healing. But none of them could have happened if she hadn't first used the miracle key. She put the key in the lock, forgave the man who had been responsible for this devastation and opened the door of her life to the power of God.

Today she is healed, no longer registered disabled and happily married! She was willing to pray the most powerful prayer on Earth, and the power of God to heal was released into her life. If Lynda had remained bitter and unforgiving, she would still be disabled and without hope of any real future.

Jim was five years old and was playing on the top of a trailer loaded with hay. His dad said, "Jump into my arms." Jim jumped, but his dad cruelly stepped aside and let him land on the concrete. Jim's chest was crushed by the fall. Forty-six years later he was still an asthmatic, never having been able to breathe properly since that terrible day in early childhood.

When Jim forgave his dad, God opened the floodgates of healing. Today, ten years later, he is still totally healed of the asthma that formerly crippled his breathing.

Bad things like this and accidents happen every day somewhere in the world. If one has happened to you and as a result you have been robbed of health and strength, have you ever thought of forgiving those who were responsible?

The effects on your health of bad things that have happened to you can be devastating, but refusing to forgive the people responsible will only make things worse! Choose to forgive them now, without condition, and the ropes of pain will be cut.

It's Time to Take Action!

There are many other ways in which people can steal from you. Later I will explain exactly what to do to be free of the pain of having these things stolen. But in case you want to start now to deal with some of the thieves and the robbers, I recommend that you spend a few minutes thinking through your life and asking God to show you all the times that bad circumstances have robbed you. Then for each event, ask yourself honestly if there are people associated with it whom you still need to forgive. Write down their names on a piece of paper. As you look at the list, remind yourself of the facts that these things are all in the past and that the only person who will continue to be hurt by them if you choose not to forgive is you!

Then simply express out loud your forgiveness to each person on the list one by one. For some people, you might also want to pick up the phone and speak it out or to write them a letter. For others, such as a sexual abuser, this would be very inappropriate, since it could be seen by the abuser as a fresh opportunity to engage in an ungodly relationship.

Just do whatever you feel is necessary to wipe the slate clean between you and them. God will cut those chains and melt the superglue, and you will begin to walk free!

After you've expressed your forgiveness, shred the piece of paper or put a match to it; as you do so, pray the most powerful prayer on Earth from your heart: "Father, forgive them." It's all over!

Chapter 7

Me, Too?

The Need to Forgive Ourselves

When talking about the mistakes of the past—and we've all made lots—many people begin their story with the words "I'll never forgive myself for . . ." Often, they even have faced what others have done to them, made right choices to forgive, worked through the process of and faced all the emotions of what happened.

But there still remains one huge obstacle to their healing: themselves! They manage to forgive everyone else under the sun, but somehow or other the guilt and burden of their own mistakes seem so huge that forgiving themselves has become an impossibility.

Sometimes, when terrible mistakes have been made, often with very painful consequences, the sense of loss can be enormous. The mistake may have caused an awful accident, even leading, for example, to the death of a child. It may have been a relationship that should never have been pursued, a financial involvement that went wrong and a lot of money was lost or any of a thousand and one other personal mistakes we could have made with potentially lifelong consequences.

It's Up to You!

It is true that the past cannot be changed, but it is also true that how you handle the future is in your hands. It is even possible to learn vital lessons from the mistakes of the past, lessons that can be a great blessing to you in the future.

Jesus died so that we might be forgiven. So if you hold on to the personal guilt attached to these things and refuse to forgive yourself, you are almost saying that what Jesus did for you wasn't good enough.

If, as a child, you longed to receive some sweets from your daddy but your fist was tightly clenched, you could receive nothing in your hand! By keeping your fist closed, as opposed to your hand open, you would have deprived yourself of the goodies.

Often, people who refuse to forgive themselves yearn for God to heal them of all that has happened in the past, but they go to God with their spiritual fists tightly closed. By their own choice they forfeit many of the blessings that God longs to give.

What Amazing Love!

Sometimes, refusing to forgive yourself is choosing to punish yourself for what has happened. You don't actually believe you deserve to be forgiven, so you hold yourself in personal condemnation. You make a choice to deprive yourself of life, because you believe that's all you deserve. But that's not how God sees it.

Peter, Jesus' disciple, went down this road. Three times he told people he had nothing to do with Jesus because of fear of what might happen to him (see John 18). In reality he betrayed Jesus by telling lies, even though in his heart he loved Jesus so much he couldn't bear the thought of not being as close to Him as possible when Jesus was suffering.

Simon must have been filled with personal remorse at the terrible thing he had done. As a result he did what many of us would have done—he withdrew to somewhere really safe where he could indulge his self-pity. For Simon that was in his boat, fishing on the Sea of Galilee (see John 21).

But Jesus knew what Simon Peter was going through. So after the Resurrection, Jesus sought him out and three times asked him the very simple but profound question, "Do you love Me?" For each time that Simon Peter had betrayed Jesus, Simon was given the opportunity to tell Jesus he loved Him.

For Simon this was probably the most important healing moment in his life. If Jesus had not sought him out, Simon Peter would have probably spent the rest of his days rowing around the Sea of Galilee, wallowing in self-pity and wondering what might have been.

Like Simon Peter, we can all make mistakes. In this situation the most important question for Jesus was not "What did you do?" but "Do you love Me?" When we are open to receive His love for us and express our own in return, the healing power of God goes right to the heart. God begins to heal us from the inside out! Love melts pain.

All Wrapped Up!

You may have forgiven other people and, therefore, have been freed of the control that had been in your life from others who had hurt you. But when you refuse God's love for you, you are still in bondage. You have substituted the bondage of control by others with a self-imposed bondage and have wrapped yourself in so much self-condemnation that you are unable to function properly or relate normally with others!

There is a special service available at some airports for those who are worried that their suitcase may not make the journey in one piece. For a small fee you can have your baggage completely encased in layer upon layer of tightly wrapped polyethylene. When the process is finished, the suitcase looks like a corpse wrapped in plastic graveclothes! There is no way anything can come out or anyone can get in!

One day, as I watched these plastic-coated suitcases going round and round on the baggage carousel at London's Heathrow Airport, it crossed my mind that this is what people must look like when they refuse to forgive themselves. It's as if they are wrapped in spiritual plastic, and no one can get in or out!

Living in unforgiveness toward yourself will neither change your past nor improve your future. It will only limit your potential to fulfill the very best that God still has in store for you.

Yes, we do have to deal with the consequences of personal mistakes and sin. Relationships with God and human beings need to be restored through confession and repentance. Restitution may also have to be made. But once these things have happened we must learn to walk away from the mess and not keep on going back to wallow in the mud of our own mistakes.

Hippopotamuses can wallow deep in mud for days on end. They love it; it's part of their natural environment. But people are capable of wallowing in their personal mud for a lifetime! God didn't intend for people to live like hippos! Mud is not our natural spiritual environment! We must leave the mud behind and enjoy living in the freedom that only living God's way can bring.

We need to forgive ourselves and pray the most powerful prayer on Earth for ourselves, not just for other people.

Chapter 8

How Often, Lord?

Peter's Most Important Lesson

Peter had a problem! He knew what Jesus had taught about forgiveness but, like every other human being, in his heart he was struggling and was looking for a bit of common sense to prevail. Maybe there was some particular person Peter really struggled with, and he was looking for an excuse to hang on to just a bit of unforgiveness!

Surely, there has to be a limit, he must have thought. *You don't really expect me to keep on forgiving forever, do You? Especially when people keep on doing the same thing to me time and time again?*

So, ever-generous Simon came up with his own answer to the problem and put it to Jesus as a proposal that he hoped would settle the matter once and for all! He was keen to get a ruling from Jesus as to what the limit was! "How about seven times, Lord? Surely no one deserves to be forgiven more often than that?"

No Limits

I would love to have seen the gentle smile on Jesus' face. It's probable that when He answered the question, neither Peter nor the rest of the disciples were prepared for His challenging answer, "Not seven times, Peter, but seventy times seven!" (see Matt. 18:22).

If you are quick at arithmetic, you will have realized by now that 490 is considerably more than Simon's 7! But in reality, Jesus was not proposing that Simon, or anybody else for that matter, should keep a long list of the number of times someone had been forgiven and then, when he had chocked up 490 in the record books, was free to do what he liked.

The Jewish colloquial phrase "seventy times seven" actually means a number so big that you don't even think about starting to count. In His reply to Simon's question, therefore, Jesus put no actual limit on the number of times Simon had to be willing to forgive!

The shocking truth is that if there is a limit on the number of times we are willing to forgive others, then there will also have to be a limit on the number of times God is able to forgive us—the consequences of which none of us would ever wish to contemplate!

Remember what Jesus said in the Lord's Prayer: "Forgive us our trespasses, as we forgive those who trespass against us" (see Matt. 6:12). In this extraordinary prayer Jesus first introduced the idea that our forgiveness by God could be related to our willingness to forgive others.

Since none of us would ever want there to be a limit on God's willingness to forgive us, there cannot be a limit on the number of times we must be willing to forgive others, no matter what they have done!

This might be easier for us to understand and accept if we remember that forgiveness has nothing to do with whether someone deserves to be forgiven—it is an act of love, not of justice.

Broken Trust

Neither does forgiveness have anything to do with future trust. A forgiven person may still be an untrustworthy person.

Sadly, many people have made the mistake of thinking that not only do they have to forgive but that their forgiveness also requires them to continue to trust that person as if nothing had happened. This is not the case and, in some cases, can be very dangerous.

I knew of a man who had been discovered sexually abusing a friend's children, whom he babysat. He seemed deeply repentant when he was found out, full of remorse and heartbreak at what he had done. Initially he was suspended from his job in the church, but then he was forgiven by both the church leaders and the child's parents.

So, as part of the forgiveness process he was given back his job as a teacher in the Sunday School. It wasn't long before it was discovered that he was abusing more children. To put him back in his old job, facing such temptation, had been a terrible mistake. He should not have been trusted in this way.

When a person has sinned against another human being, they have broken trust, both with man and God. The offer of forgiveness does not always mean that trust has been restored. In most cases trust has to be earned.

And in situations such as this one, it would never be wise to put such a person back in a place where an obvious weakness possibly could lead to further abuse.

Complete Forgiveness

When you read the account of Simon's question and Jesus' answer, it is usually assumed that the need to forgive over and over is because someone keeps on doing the same thing. But, in my experience, there is another much more commonly encountered situation that requires repeated forgiveness.

When a person has been severely traumatized by the events in his or her life and the consequential damage has been very great, there may be many levels of pain locked away in the memories.

The first time a person forgives is often an act of the will, which is contrary to the real, deeply buried feelings he or she may have. But then the feelings begin to surface—like waves on the seashore, seemingly without end.

In cases like this, every time a memory comes to the surface is another opportunity to forgive. Slowly the waves will subside, but someone may even need to forgive in excess of 490 times before the last amount of pain has been dissipated and forgiveness is complete.

Complete Freedom

How often do I have to forgive, Lord? The real answer is until there is no longer any need to forgive and all the pain has been dealt with. At that point you have, with God's help, won a major victory in your life.

No longer will the chains of bondage from the past be able to hold you fast. You will be free once again to become the person God intended. For the rest of your life you will be able to fulfill the destiny that God has reserved for you.

Jesus was clearly concerned about the effect unforgiveness would have on His disciples, including you and me. If He had put a limit on the number of times we had to forgive, there would also be a limit on the freedom that we would experience through forgiving others.

Consider Pauline's experience with forgiveness: She had to forgive many times before she was able to be free of the sexual abuse that was done to her as a child. Too frightened to sleep on a bed at night because of what might happen to her, Pauline had for twenty years slept on the floor under the bed. She felt safe there.

Pauline took an enormous step of courageous faith when she made that first faltering move towards forgiving those responsible. It was a step that saved her life. As the memories surfaced, she had to forgive time and time again, but every time she forgave, it was as if God were removing another layer of grave clothes from her personality.

Pauline is only alive today because she learned Simon Peter's lesson—there can be no limit to forgiveness! She was one who truly prayed the most powerful prayer on Earth, "Father, forgive." It was the miracle key she had been looking for, not only to overcome all the inner anger at what others had done, but also to know the love of Jesus in quite an extraordinary way.

Few people will suffer such awful things as Pauline did. Today you can know for certain that what God did for Pauline, He can do for you.

Chapter 9

What About God?

The Need to Say We're Sorry to God for Blaming Him

Deborah winced with pain as she tried to knock the stuffing out of a cushion with her fist. "Surely, if God really is God, He could have stopped all the bad things that have happened to me." Her anger was surfacing, and God was the target as she forcefully expressed her feelings to her counselors!

Deborah was asking a very valid question. If God is as loving and all-powerful as Christians say He is, then why does He sit in heaven, watching all sorts of terrible things happen on Earth, and do nothing about them? It doesn't make sense. "I'm not sure I want to know a God like that," Deborah added.

There was nothing wrong with her logic, and her feelings were totally understandable. But she was missing a few facts in the argument, which had led to a major distortion in her thinking and understanding.

Free Will

The first fact that Deborah did not understand is that we are made in the image and likeness of God. Among other important things, this means that we, like God, have free will. We were made with the capacity to make choices of our own.

If we had no capacity to exercise free will, then we would have no capacity to choose what relationships we enter into. Without free will, our lives would be reduced to the level of robots. The joy of choice is key to personal enjoyment and pleasure.

Every human being is unique. We enjoy different things. Some people prefer pizza to hamburgers. Others love chicken. For vacation some people like to be by the sea, others prefer the mountains. Some love talking about politics while others prefer to play active sports. Variety and choice are central to our way of life.

No matter what our preferences may be, we have the freedom to choose what we like. Take away free will, and life as we know it ceases to exist. But having free will—without the recognition of safe boundaries—can be very dangerous!

Safe Boundaries

It was using free will to go outside the boundaries set by God that landed humankind in a mess in the first place! We chose to question what God had said and to rebel against the God who had made us. The rest, as they say, is history!

In what is generally referred to as the Fall, we willingly put ourselves under an ungodly authority. Ever since, that ungodly authority has done everything possible to destroy the relationship between God and humankind by encouraging one generation after another to dispense with godly order and go beyond the limits of God's boundaries.

We have seen that process happen in our own generation. The scriptural standards of morality, for example, which have formed the backbone of law and order in most Western nations for hundreds of years, have now virtually all been swept away by a rising tide of immorality, amorality and sexual promiscuity.

When young children go outside the safe boundaries their parents provide, they quickly get into danger. For this reason, parents provide the safety of a playpen for their two-year-olds. And if people could go where and how they liked on the roads, there would be innumerable accidents, so our authorities provide rules and boundaries for traffic so that people can drive to places in safety without the risk of a head-on collision.

Every year in Canada people go out on frozen lakes to enjoy themselves, and some lose their lives in the process! A frozen lake provides a wonderful and safe facility for the thrill of traveling at high speed across the ice on a snowmobile —provided, that is, people stay within the areas where the ice is known to be sufficiently thick for safety.

But every year there are some people who think they know better than the authorities and go beyond the recommended boundaries. Every year there are families who are forced to mourn the loss of adventuresome or foolhardy explorers who thought they knew best and went beyond the boundaries.

It's a bit like that with God's boundaries also. The rebellion and independence within us make us want to live beyond the safety of the rules and boundaries provided by a loving and caring God.

People have failed to understand that the Ten Commandments, for example, were not given by God to stop them from enjoying themselves but to provide safe boundaries within which they can exercise free will without getting into danger.

Evil and the Evil One

The Bible calls going beyond these boundaries trespassing, or sinning. The consequence of using our free will to make sinful choices is that evil is given the opportunity to increase its influence in our lives.

In the Lord's Prayer, Jesus encourages us to pray, "Deliver us from evil" (Matt. 6:13, *NASB*) or, more accurately, "Deliver us from the evil one." There is an evil "god of this world" (2 Cor. 4:4, *NASB*) who opposes every good thing that God prepared for His children.

When we pray this portion of the Lord's Prayer, we are asking God to help us make right choices so that we will be kept safe within God's boundaries. We are also praying for protection from the evil one, who from the beginning has used his free will in the spiritual realms to tempt man to do wrong things and to oppose the living God. The Bible calls him Satan (see Matt. 4:10).

Our Blameless God

In reality, then, all the bad things that happen in this world are not God's fault. They are the consequences of the influence of the evil one and the wrong choices that people make as a result of his influence. We should not blame God for things that He is not responsible for.

If God were to use His ultimate power and authority to put a stop to everything that He doesn't like, then He would have to take away our free will and put a stop to most of what is going on in the world. We would no longer be human beings capable of free-will relationships with each other and with the capacity to choose to enjoy a free-will relationship with God.

The Bible tells us that Father God loved us so much that He willingly sent His Son, Jesus, to show us how much He loves us and wants to have a restored relationship with His children (see John 3:16-17).

We live in a fallen, and consequently evil, world. We only have to read one newspaper or listen to one news bulletin to realize what a mess humankind has made of this world that God created.

Instead of blaming God for what humankind and the evil one have done, an important step toward healing from the curse of bitterness—which comes as a by-product of unforgiveness—is to say to God that we're sorry for blaming Him for things that were not His fault.

Saying we're sorry to God is another vital key to healing. Use it and it will remove a major obstacle that may be keeping you from being able to forgive others and to pray the most powerful prayer on Earth.

Chapter 10

The Seven Steps to Freedom
Instructions for Using God's Miracle Key

Your future is in your and God's hands! No matter how much the first part of your life has been messed up, you and God together can change your destiny so that in the second part of your life you are free to become the person God intended and to know the blessing of God in a new way. The rest of your life begins today!

King David wrote of the wonderful blessings God promises to those who understand the boundaries that God has set and who gladly choose to walk within them. Here is what David wrote:

The law of the LORD is perfect, *reviving the soul.*
The statutes of the LORD are trustworthy, *making wise the simple.*
The precepts of the LORD are right, *giving joy to the heart.*
The commands of the LORD are radiant, *giving light to the eyes.*
The fear of the LORD is pure, *enduring forever.*
The ordinances of the LORD are *sure and altogether righteous.*

They are *more precious than gold,* than much pure gold;
they are *sweeter than honey,* than honey from the comb.
By them is your servant warned; *in keeping them there is great
   reward.*

(Ps. 19:7-11, emphasis added)

In His Word, God has given wonderful guidelines for
living. He has also shown where the dangers are. And in
this amazing psalm God promises that if you choose to live
within the boundaries He has set (the law of the Lord), He
will revive your soul, give you His wisdom, give joy to your
heart, put light in your eyes, warn you of danger and enable
you to enjoy His reward! *What wonderful promises!*

When I look into the eyes of the many hurting people
who come to me for help, so often I see the very opposite of
all these wonderful blessings that God promises to those who
follow Him. I can see hurt, disappointment, pain, anger,
resentment, bitterness and many other negative responses to
the experiences of life.

One of the most important laws that God has shown us
in His Word is the law of sowing and reaping. Paul tells
us that we can't ignore God's counsel and not expect there
to be consequences. In one of his letters Paul put it this
way: "God cannot be mocked. A man reaps what he sows"
(Gal. 6:7).

This means that whatever sort of seed we sow in our life, it
will eventually produce a harvest in keeping with the nature
of the seed. In the context of this book, therefore, it means
that if we sow unforgiveness, we will reap bitterness. And if
we continue to sow the same seed throughout our days, bitterness will give rise to many harmful consequences in our
own life and in the lives of those we relate to day by day.
These consequences could even include physical symptoms
and conditions.

"So what must I do," I hear you saying, "if I don't want to grow this kind of crop in my life?"

If you've already recognized your own need of forgiveness and decided to believe in Jesus and trust your life to Him, you've already taken one huge step forward. You are already at a new place in God from which you can take another huge step forward and begin to know God's healing and reap the benefits of learning to pray the most powerful prayer on Earth.

Now is the time to get practical and understand the steps you need to take in order to apply this wonderful teaching of Scripture in your own life.

Step 1—Make a Decision

We have already understood together that God has given to each one of us free will—the capacity to make choices.

So the first step you need to take is to look back at every difficult situation there has ever been in your life and make a choice to forgive, without condition, everyone who was involved in them. This is your decision and yours alone. No one else can do it for you!

I was asked to pray for a woman named Jane. Twenty-four years prior, Jane was riding on the back of a two-man snow-mobile on frozen Lake Ontario. Paul, the driver, lost control, and the machine somersaulted many times on the ice. Jane was thrown around like a rag doll as her body flew across the ice, her head banging repeatedly on the iron-hard surface.

Ever since, Jane has suffered with major physical problems affecting her spine, her joints and her shoulders. She has had years of medical and chiropractic treatment with no permanent benefit or relief.

As we began to pray for her physical problems, I was prompted to ask, "Have you forgiven Paul?" It was obvious from the look on her face that she hadn't forgiven the man who had caused her twenty-four years of pain.

It was clear that Jane had some serious work to do with God, so I said that I couldn't pray for her until she had overcome this important obstacle. Some time passed before she was able to come to the place of choosing to forgive Paul and release him into the freedom of her forgiveness.

It had to be her choice. No amount of praying for her condition at that stage would have helped her. If I had started to pray for her physical problems while her unforgiveness was creating a barrier to the love and power of God, nothing would have happened, and she might have gone away thinking that God doesn't love her or that God can't or won't heal her condition.

When I was able to pray for her again, the power of God was very evidently present to heal, and twenty-four years of pain and spinal distortion were eliminated in a matter of minutes.

The following day she was radiant, having gone for a run early in the morning and having done exercises that would previously have been impossible. She was a totally different person!

Jane's physical healing came down to whether or not she was willing to make a choice to forgive. Until she had made that choice, God could do nothing!

Now it's your turn. Think about it. Are you willing to make the same choice Jane made and, whatever it costs and whatever the consequences, decide to forgive every single person who has ever hurt you, stolen something from your life, abused you, betrayed you, talked ill of you or hurt you in any other way?

To make this choice is your first step toward being able to pray the most powerful prayer on Earth and beginning to reap a new crop of blessings in your life.

Step 2—Make a List

If you have now made the choice to forgive, it is time to get out a piece of paper and start making a list. Before you get to work, pray a short prayer. You can use your own words or say something like this:

> *Thank You, Jesus, for teaching me the importance of forgiving others. Please help me to remember all the people who have hurt me so that I can forgive them from my heart.*

Prayers like this one don't have to be long or terribly formal —God is interested in you as a person and in the decisions of your heart, not in whether or not you are good with words!

One way of making your list is to think through your life. You can begin at the beginning and work forward or you can start from where you are and work backward—it doesn't matter which.

Whichever direction you decide to go, the two names that need to be at the top of your list are your parents'—even if you think they were perfect! In reality no parents were ever perfect, and they may also have carried to you problems caused by what their parents and grandparents had done. (You may also need to repent of any ungodly reactions you had to things your parents did—there are two sides to every relationship!)

Be careful and systematic, and give God a chance to remind you of people you might have forgotten. Every time you think of someone you need to forgive, write down his or her name. You may also find it helpful to write down the particular reason for which you need to forgive that person. You need to ask God to remind you of things that may have happened in your family, with your friends and with any other circle of people with whom you have shared something of your life over the years. Think back on every year of your life and everywhere you've been—school, work, church, sports events, vacations, and so on. Don't rush it—give yourself space and time.

And don't forget to put your own name on the list if you struggle with the consequences of mistakes you have made or have ever cursed yourself by saying something like "I'll never forgive myself!"

Some names will cause you more pain than others, and you might even have difficulty writing down some of the names. Inside you might think that you don't want to forgive them or they don't deserve to be forgiven.

If you have difficulties like this, look back to the specific chapter in this book that deals with the particular problem you are having, read it again and be determined to press on. Remember, you've made a decision to forgive, so ask God to help you write down the names!

Step 3—Start to Forgive

Now's the time for another short prayer. Pray something like this:

> *Lord Jesus, thank You for dying on the cross that I might be forgiven. I am sorry for my own sins, and I ask You to be my Savior and the Lord of my life. And now please forgive me for the things that I have done wrong. Please help me to forgive from my heart all the people on my list.*

Then as you go down the list pray carefully over each name. Remind yourself for a moment about what it was they did to you, and then pray something like this:

> *I now choose to forgive* [insert the name of the person you are forgiving] *for* [insert a brief description of what was done to you], *and I release* [insert the person's name] *into the freedom of my forgiveness. I will not hold these things against* [insert the person's name] *any more.*

As you pray through your list from your heart, you will find that God slowly changes you from the inside out. You will be leaving behind all the bad things that resentment and bitterness have brought into your life and begin to emerge like a butterfly at the beginning of a new era.

Step 4—Ask God to Set You Free

You can do this after each prayer of forgiveness or you can say it at the end about everyone you've forgiven. Whichever way you choose, pray something like this:

Thank You, Lord, for helping me forgive [insert the name of the person you are forgiving]. *I ask now that You set me free from every ungodly influence that* [insert the person's name] *has had on my life and that You cut the ropes that have held me tightly to the pain of the past.*

Step 5—Say You're Sorry for Blaming God

If at various times of your life you have blamed God for things that you now know were not His responsibility, you will want to tell Him you are sorry and ask Him to forgive you before you move on. You can use words like these:

I'm sorry, God, for blaming You for the bad things that have happened in my life. I now know You did not want these things to happen either. Please forgive me.

Step 6—Pray the Most Powerful Prayer on Earth

Praying the most powerful prayer on Earth is what this book is all about! We have had to travel quite a journey through your life to get to this point. When Jesus prayed, "Father, forgive them, for they do not know what they are doing," there was no sin, unforgiveness, resentment, bitterness or ungodly anger in His heart, so He didn't have to do what you have just done.

Jesus was free to be able to pray this most amazing prayer with a pure heart, right in the middle of His own pain. I wonder what thoughts the Roman soldiers had as they nailed Him to the cross and heard His prayer?

I said earlier in this book that forgiveness is an act of love, not of justice. The heart of Jesus toward His accusers and killers was a heart of love. Above all else He wanted all men and women to be able to come to know God and to experience God's forgiveness for themselves.

Jesus' disciples must have wondered what He really meant when He taught them, "Love your enemies, do good to those who hate you, bless those who curse you, pray for those who mistreat you" (Luke 6:27-28). Now they knew. Here was Jesus putting His own teaching into practice as He prayed, "Father, forgive them."

Jesus died with these words on His lips and in His heart. He had given no ground to His accusers, and as a result neither the evil one nor any of the powers of darkness could touch Him. *This was the most powerful prayer on Earth because it led to Resurrection morning!*

The final stage in offering forgiveness to others, therefore, is to pray, as Jesus did, that those who have hurt you will be forgiven for everything they have done. Of course, you cannot pray such a prayer with an honest heart until you have first forgiven people for what they have done to you. When you forgive, God will release healing into the consequences of your past and will work miracles that will transform every area of your life.

To go one step further and pray as Jesus did is to make a choice to bless selflessly the lives of others—yes, even those who have hurt you! By so doing you are following the example of Jesus and helping others have the opportunity to know God for themselves and to respond to His love. This is the greatest blessing we can ever bestow on others.

Those you have forgiven have free will regarding how they will respond to what God does in their life as a result of your prayer. You are not responsible for any choices they make.

Corrie ten Boom became famous for her and her family's work in preserving the lives of over 800 Jews who were being pursued by the Nazis during World War II. Four members of her family gave their lives because of their commitment.

Corrie's sister, Betsy, died just before the end of the war in the Ravensbruck death camp, but Corrie survived. When Corrie came home, she realized that her life was a gift from God and that she needed to share, not how awful her accusers had been, but what she and Betsy had learned in Ravensbruck: "There is no pit so deep that God's love is not deeper still," and "God will give us the love to be able to forgive our enemies."[1]

Corrie had learned to use God's miracle key in one of Earth's darkest places! And so, at age fifty-three, she entered an era of great blessing as she began a worldwide ministry that took her into more than sixty countries in the next thirty-two years![2]

There was nothing from Corrie's past that could hold her in chains of bondage—God's miracle key had set her free!

The family of Stephen Oake also learned to pray the most powerful prayer on Earth. Stephen was an outstanding Christian policeman serving in the Greater Manchester (England) Police Force. In January 2003, he was tragically killed in the line of duty when a suspect turned on his captors and stabbed Stephen to death. Stephen left behind grieving parents, a heartbroken wife and young children.

Stephen's father, a retired senior police officer, and Stephen's wife were quick to speak out to the press and television reporters forgiveness of the man who had done this terrible thing, which had robbed the family of a son, a husband and a father.

This was a very high-profile incident in the United Kingdom. The nation was stunned, not only by the tragedy itself, but also by the family's genuine Christian reaction to what had happened. The fruit of this remarkable response has been to free the family of the chains of bitterness and provide some very significant opportunities for sharing the gospel with others—especially among the police officers themselves.

Not only does God's miracle key, the most powerful prayer on Earth, have an effect on those you have prayed for, but it also opens the door for God to pour His blessing on your own life in a new way. *You can no longer be chained to the past by anyone who has hurt you. You are free!*

So ask Jesus now to give you His love for all those who have hurt you and quietly pray,

Father, forgive them.

Let it become the most powerful prayer on Earth for you as well.

Step 7—Expect Your Resurrection Morning

When Jesus rose from the dead and burst out of the tomb, He was no longer wearing the grave clothes in which His body had been wrapped. As you break out from the chains of your past, the transformation for you will be like a Resurrection morning in your life.

Jesus promised to make all things new (see 2 Cor. 5:17; Rev. 21:5). The grave clothes of bitterness will be gone, and God's divine law of blessing will start to operate in your life.

As you speak out your forgiveness to all those people whose names are on your list and then pray, "Father, forgive them," your life will begin to be changed forever. *There is a Resurrection morning coming for you as well!*

Notes

1. Corrie ten Boom Foundation, E. Smith, "History," *Corrie ten Boom Museum.* http://www.corrietenboom.com/history.htm (accessed December 30, 2003).

2. Ibid.

Chapter 11

It's Up to You!
Final Thoughts

Your life is unique. All that has happened to you since the moment you were conceived is your own personal story. It will remain your own story—yours and yours alone—until the day you die and leave this world behind. The same is true for the rest of your life. What happens to you between now and when you die matters more to you than to anyone else in the world.

Your life has only two parts: the part you've already lived and the part yet to be lived. The first part is always getting longer and the second part is always getting shorter!

All of us want to enjoy and make the most of whatever time we have left to live on this planet. What you do now could make the difference between being blessed out of your socks for the rest of your life or struggling to keep your head above water in a sea of disappointment, resentment, bitterness and even anger, hatred or revenge.

The sooner you really understand that there is a direct connection between how you respond now to the difficult moments of the first part of your life and how much you are able to enjoy and be fulfilled in this second part, the sooner you will be able to start living your life again to the full. When the ropes of unforgiveness have been well and truly cut, there is nothing that can keep you bound to the pain of your past.

No good whatsoever is being served by hanging on to memories of bitterness, no matter what others may have done. The longer you hang on to them, the more the second part of your life is being eaten into by the first. Every day you spend in unforgiveness pushes the cost up and gives the past a right to haunt you in the present!

The Bible is full of promises of restoration and hope for the people of God. But there are always conditions attached to the promises of God, and one of those conditions is choosing to forgive. So what's stopping you? You have absolutely nothing to lose and everything to gain!

The amazing prayer that Jesus prayed truly was the most powerful prayer on Earth. You can start praying it now and begin to experience God's presence, love and power in your life in a new way.

The key is in your hand. It's a key of miracles. But only you can use it. Let this first day of the rest of your life be the beginning of a new era of blessing for you. Now is the time to act!

I personally pray that as you think carefully about the contents of this book and as you resolve to use the miracle key, God will meet you at your point of need and you will know the transforming power of His love and forgiveness for yourself.

PART 2

I TURNED THE MASTER KEY!

Chapter 12

Personal Stories of Healing Through Forgiveness

For more than twenty years I have been teaching about forgiveness and ministering to people who have come to our Centers for help. In the early days I quickly discovered that forgiveness is, perhaps, the most important element in anyone's pilgrimage towards wholeness. That was certainly what Jesus must have thought, for Him to have spoken out so strongly about the consequences of not forgiving others in Matthew 6:15.

Those years of ministry are for me like a long corridor of time—with pictures framed on its walls showing the people whom God touched deeply on a healing retreat, a training course, at a conference or in a personal ministry appointment.

I can see many of them now in my mind as I write these words—people who I will never forget because of what God did in their lives. Some of their stories are already included in the first part of *Forgiveness—God's Master Key*. In this second part of the book I want to share a few more of those memories.

Then I want to allow some of those faces to come off the wall and share for themselves something of what God did in their lives, as they turned the forgiveness master key and discovered that the Master Himself was right there, ready to bring His wonderful healing into the very depths of their lives.

Some had suffered great rejection, even by their own Mum or Dad, others had been sexually abused. Yet others had been injured in accidents that were not their fault. Some had been betrayed or robbed. And, sadly, some of these problems had been caused by people they thought they could trust, even fellow Christians or members of their own family. The catalogue of possible pain in the lives of human beings is longer than most people's capacity to imagine what people can suffer.

It sometimes seems as though their whole life has been destroyed by what has happened and there seems little hope for their future. And yet, for all these people, there is one key they can turn, which will begin the process of healing from the past, and transform both their present and their future. They have to turn God's master key and forgive those who have hurt them.

Frida's Story

On occasions their story has been so horrendous, you wonder if it would ever be possible for a human being to forgive in those circumstances. I will never forget a young woman from Rwanda introducing herself at the beginning of one of our training schools at Ellel Grange.

She radiated the beauty of Jesus, but she bore the scars of the Rwandan genocide in 1994, when a million Tutsi people were killed by Hutus in a tribal war in just 100 days. Frida was the only surviving member of her immediate family. On one day all her fifteen close relatives—including grandparents, parents, brothers and sisters—were gathered together in one place and asked how they wanted to die. If you were wealthy enough to buy your own bullet you could be shot and get it over with quickly. Frida's family were poor. Her mother chose the machete and Frida herself chose to be hit over the back of the head with a blunt instrument—she thought that would be quick.

One by one all her family were executed, including Frida, and pushed into a shallow grave. But Frida wasn't actually dead. She was buried alive and covered over. Fourteen hours later someone heard a sound from the grave and dug her out. Some time later, when the genocide was all over, she became a Christian and started to read the Bible. There she read about forgiveness and knew she had to do what Jesus said and go to the jail to forgive the man who had killed her father.

That act freed her from the consequences of bitterness and any possibility of a desire for revenge. Without forgiveness she would have been in bondage to the people who had done those terrible things for the rest of her days. At Ellel Grange she spoke out again her forgiveness to everyone who had been involved in those terrible events. Till that time she had been suffering awful nightmares and constant pain in the head in the place where she had been hit. That night God healed her completely. She was freed from the pain and from the recurring nightmares. Her full remarkable story is told in her book *Frida—Chosen to Die, Destined to Live*, published by Sovereign World.

Today she is married to a pastor in Kigali, the capital city of Rwanda, where together she and her husband are ministering hope and healing to their own people. Frida not only found her own healing when she turned God's master key, but subsequently many hundreds, if not thousands, of her people will be able to join in the experience of being blessed through the process of forgiveness.

When people tell me that the events in their particular story are too hard to forgive, I tell them Frida's story. For Frida her healing began with a choice—a choice to forgive, no matter how hard it is. But then people discover that God gives His grace to carry out the choice they have made.

John's Story

John's story was different, but he still had to begin at the same place—forgiving those who had rejected him and subjected him to a regime of fear and pain. This is what he said:

> God has transformed my life. I came from a background of rejection, fear, pain, violence, hate, drug addiction, homosexuality, prostitution, occultism and depression. When I met the Holy Spirit my life completely changed and God has used Ellel Ministries in such a way that has allowed me to see deeper into my life and has brought true healing and deliverance.
>
> Now I have my life back. I finally feel that I am living again. The love of God has changed me and I am free. I have found the purpose I am here for.

Simon's Story

Simon described how he had personally used the master key of forgiveness and entered into an arena of life that, previously, would have been impossible for him.

> Walking down the road of forgiveness has been a key to unlocking the treasures of heaven in my life. It is a key that opens the gates of heaven for God's blessings to be outpoured. He is so faithful.
>
> Forgiving someone is not about taking away the responsibility from the people who hurt me, or giving the impression that the

act of violation was somehow OK. It is about releasing it all into the hands of God, and letting Him be the judge of everything. As challenging and painful as this road undeniably is, His mercy and gentleness is far greater.

A step of obedience is always followed by the healing touch of the Holy Spirit, so sweet and tender yet so fair and so just. I am allowed to see my own weaknesses and what my sins have caused others and I know He carried my guilt as well on the cross. Glory be to God for the cross of Jesus!

I pray that there will always be those who choose to travel on this road. It is the road of the Kingdom of God, where the Prince of Peace rules. No powers of darkness can prevail against it. He truly brought me out into the open landscapes where I can lie down and rest. Be assured, He does redeem the years that the locust has eaten. His thoughts and plans for me are always for good and not for evil.

Linda's Story

Many of those who face the deepest pain have been sexually abused. And when the abuse has been caused by your own father it is especially unbearable. When a father violates that position of trust that God put him in, by using and abusing his own daughter, it causes damage that can take half a lifetime to face and, sadly, many of those who suffered the most never find the answer that only Jesus can provide.

Linda was one of those whose very life was in the balance when she came to Ellel for help. She had had years of medical help for her broken life. But there was nothing more the doctors could do. Yet when you hear her story you will be able to rejoice at the miracle-working power of God that is released in a person's life through forgiveness. She truly turned the master key and saw God rescue her from the miry clay and put her feet on a rock.

My father sexually abused me throughout my childhood, and although my mother knew what was happening, she didn't try to protect me. In fact she was angry and withheld her love from me. I took all the blame on myself, and grew up full of guilt and self-hatred. I became depressed and suicidal and eventually ended up in a psychiatric hospital.

Mercifully God had a rescue plan for my life, which began to unfold when I was given the opportunity to receive Christian counseling and ministry. I learned that a big key to healing was forgiveness, and I realized I needed to forgive my parents for the cruelty they had rained on me. To begin with, it wasn't something I struggled with. Jesus had given the instruction in the Bible, so I obeyed.

But I didn't experience any great sense of release. I was still so afraid of people that I wouldn't go outside and hid when anyone came to the house. I still hated myself intensely and battled with suicidal thoughts and the desire to self-harm.

Gradually I began to understand that my forgiveness was incomplete if it didn't involve more than a mental decision detached from pain. I realized I had to feel my emotional responses to the cruelty of my childhood: the pain, anger and deep sense of injustice I had buried deep down inside myself. And in the midst of feeling the intensity of these emotions, I had to face the issue of forgiveness all over again.

My self-hatred was a defense. Believing I was bad covered the fact that it was my parents' actions towards me that were bad, and that as a child I didn't deserve to be abused.

I repented of hating myself, and gradually the Lord helped me to connect to my hidden emotions, and to embrace the truth of how I really felt. There wasn't just pain and anger, but desperate cries of, "It's not fair!" and "I wanted it to be different!" There was bitterness, resentment, a desire for revenge, and jealousy of what others had that I didn't have. The whole process was like having a dirty dressing taken off a deep festering wound.

I couldn't have faced it on my own, but this was a work of the Holy Spirit. He asked me not just to face "the truth in the innermost parts" as He enabled me, but to allow Him into the wound. My part was to take my pain to the foot of the cross, and in the midst of feeling my bitterness and unforgiveness to choose to forgive.

This was hard and it took time. I battled on the one hand with the pain of the injustice of being abused and unloved, and my stubborn resistance to forgiveness, and on the other hand with the conviction from Jesus that I needed to forgive, knowing that, wholly sinless, He had cried out, "Father, forgive them" when He was nailed to the cross.

Being brutally honest with God in the battle with my bitterness and unforgiveness, was important. I had to own that this was me, this was how I felt and I couldn't change it. It was only then that I could receive His enabling to do what was impossible for me.

I wanted to obey Him and again made a choice in my head to forgive, but it was Jesus who enabled me to forgive in my heart. Gradually I learned to take the pain and negative emotion to Him each time I felt it, and little by little He enabled me to forgive, and to receive His comfort where I needed it. What a gracious God He is!

I can truthfully say that my life is completely different today. I have an inner security and strength that comes from having allowed God into my deepest place of pain, and to have His way in that place. I no longer suffer with the fears that were once so debilitating, am free of all psychiatric medication, have been signed off a lifetime's incapacity benefit, am in paid employment, and free to fully enter into life with my family and friends in a way that I never thought could be possible. I am so thankful and give Him all the praise, all the glory and all the honor.

Johann's Story

Johann is typical of many people—people who get into bad
and dangerous habits without understanding the reason why.
They do not understand how things that happened to them
in the past can be at the root of today's problems. This is how
Johann told his story.

*I've been a sort of Christian for about ten years, but a re-born
Christian for only a year. I am praising Jesus so much for everything He has done and for leading me into a deeper relationship
with Him than I could ever have dreamt of.*

*At the age of twenty-six I got involved with wrong friends
and started using drugs (cocaine). I was using cocaine for over
two years. About then I got offered a new job with the Standard
Bank. I worked on the fifth floor next to a woman called Esther
whom I'd never met before.*

*After I'd been working in the bank for a week, she asked me
a simple question, "Are you a Christian?" I answered "yes," so
she gave me a teaching series from Peter Horrobin called "Ministering Hope." At that time I was traveling on my motorcycle
every day from Pretoria to Johannesburg. I hadn't listened to the
CDs—I thought they'd be too boring! But a few days later I had
an accident on the motorcycle, which forced me to go by car. For
some or other reason the CDs had been left in my car.*

*One day I started listening to them. It was like God talking
into my spirit. I got born again in my car on the way to work!
I realized it was time to move back into the hands of God. I
managed to quit the drugs without even going to a rehab, just
by listening to Peter's teaching.*

*God showed me how to get healed on the inside by forgiv-
ing my step-grandfather who had molested me at the age of
five—which I then knew was the cause of my unhappiness. God
showed me how important it is to get healed from the root of*

the problem where the unhappiness started. My life changed so much.

But after a few months I was in another serious motorcycle accident. I had been in a coma for two days. The accident left me with two broken knees, five broken ribs and a broken shoulder. People told me that I was the most fortunate person in the world. I learned there had been a doctor driving four cars behind me. He saw the accident happening and prevented my ribs from puncturing my lungs.

Doctors told me that they had bad news for me and that there was a chance of losing my right leg. I kept my faith in God. Now I have fully recovered from the accident without losing my leg. God is so powerful!

I could not understand why God allowed this accident because I loved Him so much and tried my best to keep in line with Him. The answer was very simple. God will never allow bad things to happen to you, but Satan makes it happen when you are out of God's governance. (I realized that I was speeding far over the speed limit.) God will take the bad thing that happened to you and change it into a good thing. I just want to praise and thank Him for helping me through this accident.

Last but not least, I was baptized on 3 Feb. 08. I thank Jesus again for this special gift in my life. God used Peter's teaching to give me a second chance in life to experience His love and faithfulness that will never ever fail.

When Johann got into drugs he was at the end of a downward spiral which had begun with the childhood molestation. Children don't know how to cope with the consequences of what's happening to them and usually they bury the pain and hurt. But pain such as this is "buried alive" and unless it is healed by Jesus, it will have its outworking—taking drugs is just one of the many coping mechanisms that people can use. But it is a path of self-destruction.

Fortunately Johann quickly got to the root of the problem after he was born again, forgave his grandfather and asked God to cut him free from this ungodly relationship. Johann turned the master key and now lives to serve his Lord.

Forgiveness and Healing in Kenya

Recently an Ellel Ministries team were conducting a training conference in Kenya. The teaching on forgiveness is always a vital part of the foundational teaching on all such missions. This is how the leader of the mission reported the event.

A pastor's wife gave a powerful testimony of the freedom she experienced after forgiving her son-in-law's family who physically and emotionally persecuted her and her husband after their daughter died at the birth of their grandchild. The forgiveness teaching was so critical to them. There were many others who needed to forgive also, so many difficult things had happened in their lives. Many were crying as they forgave. I realized yet again the importance of the forgiveness teaching in Africa, as so many people here have experienced rejection.

God did an amazing restoration in the life of the pastor. He gave testimony how he had forgiven for the first time the people who had killed his son and the release he felt. After the conference closed he brought his five-year-old son for prayer—his legs were about 4 cm uneven. God did a miracle and healed this boy's legs to be completely even! We serve a God of miracles! We truly rejoiced at God's goodness!

And also in Malaysia...

God impressed me to pray for my mum for inner healing—she had gone through a lot of rejection. She was given away as soon as she was born and even today, she doesn't know who her real parents were. She was abused by words and told she had brought bad luck to the family. At the age of sixteen she was put into a forced marriage to my father and made to work and look after my father's entire family—cooking and cleaning.

I am so thankful to God for teaching me about inner healing. Because I was healed I could help my mum. God healed and delivered her of all the pains and hurt she had been carrying for so many, many years. She will be eighty in July.

I have led my mum to repentance and helped her to be born again. Jesus helped her to remember the people she needed to forgive. She started to cry and the Holy Spirit just took over and brought deliverance and healing. God is so good!

Elaine's Story

Elaine's story is a wonderful account of how God can heal even the deepest pain—and not only heal but restore our experience of life so that every area is totally transformed by the presence of God. A master key is a key that will open every lock—God's master key is so powerful!

I have been a Christian for over twenty years and have enjoyed a wonderful walk with my Savior for many years. However, due to a series of events over the last six years or so, I was hurting so much and struggling to come to terms with them. Through this hurt, rejection, depression and confusion I looked for love and acceptance in all the wrong places, and my sinful life caused me to think I had lost my salvation.

My life became a constant struggle of trying to do the right things, yet at the same time battling with depression, loneliness, self-rejection... the list is endless. As a Christian I knew I should give it all to God, and while I know He is a fair and just God, and everything works together for good, I felt so much shame, guilt and injustice. Suicide was a constant companion and seemed to offer a way out of the pain. Thankfully, by God's mercy, the attempts that I did make were unsuccessful. Looking back, I now realize that He really does have good plans for my life.

I came for a healing retreat expecting and knowing God would do something, but never in my wildest dreams did I ever imagine He would do so much.

On a healing retreat the leaders give very practical teaching on how to truly live the Christian life. They explain about how Jesus needs to be Lord of every area of our being and, of course, a lot of space is given to helping people to forgive the people who have hurt them.

Through the excellent teaching and wonderful, sensitive counseling, the Holy Spirit revealed roots to my problems and helped me understand how these had given the enemy inroads into my life.

At the start of the retreat I explained how my life seemed like a thick unpleasant soup, all messed up. Through the Lordship prayer I was helped to separate out the different ingredients of this soup. Each ingredient was an area of my life. The Holy Spirit ministered to the areas that needed His touch. As they were dealt with, it seemed I was able to feel love like I had never known it before.

For the first time ever I knew my Heavenly Father as my Daddy, and He loved me in a way I had never encountered before. I have known of His love for many years, and I have experienced His grace and mercy more times than I will ever know, but this weekend Father God touched my heart. I realized I do not have to strive, work, perform or jump through any hoops to earn His love and approval.

I was free to see Him the way He wants me to see Him. I walked around the grounds and now the grass seemed greener, the trees were so exciting and the dawn chorus of the birds was overwhelming. I walked down the drive laughing and crying.

I had a great big smile from ear to ear. I was walking with my Daddy God and I was free to enjoy His love. I did not need to say anything. It was like we were communicating through His creation and I knew that He knew I was so happy.

Later during worship, as we sang the chorus "I have changed your name," I was overwhelmed with His love and the tears flowed and flowed. It was lovely to cry from a heart that beats once again because of God's love. I had often spoken out scriptures about God's love for me, but that weekend the knowledge of His love dropped eighteen inches from my head and really became alive in my heart!

What an extraordinary testimony of the transforming love of God—but without choosing to turn the master key, none of the joy that Elaine experienced could have been hers.

We pray for many people who have suffered the consequences of accidents. Sometimes the pain and trauma have been stored up inside for many years. Often resentment and bitterness are stored up on the inside against those who caused the accidents, severely limiting the healing process. Jim was healed of asthma after forgiving his father for deliberately letting him be crushed against a concrete floor at the age of six.

Doreen's sixteen-year battle with neck pain following a car accident was over when her neck was completely healed. Bill was not protected by his mother in the kitchen when he pulled a saucepan of boiling water down onto his chest. Forty years later God healed him of the fears and trauma which had gripped his life ever since. The list of people and circumstances is endless.

Jennifer's story is a little different—it wasn't other people that she needed to forgive. She had to use the master key to forgive herself!

Jennifer's Story

I was in a tragic car accident thirty-eight years ago when my mother and five-year-old sister were killed. Since then I have suffered from severe back pain. To try and control the pain I had to take eight strong painkillers every day.

As the team prayed with me I discovered that I was feeling guilty about the accident. At the time I had been looking after my brothers and sisters while my mum was partying. When I was asked what part of the accident I felt responsible for, I thought, "How could I be responsible for anything? I was only thirteen years old!" They encouraged me to forgive myself and, to my shock and horror, I found myself saying that I couldn't forgive myself, for in my heart I believed I was responsible for the accident because I insisted we went home. I had no problem forgiving the others, but it took me fifteen minutes to get me to a place where I could actually forgive myself.

I felt an immediate release in my physical body after they prayed over me. I was so traumatized at age thirteen by the event that something of me was locked away on the inside. I was told this often happens in severe traumas. They prayed that the Lord would heal that broken part and fully heal and restore me on the inside.

Three things have happened as a result. Firstly, I have slept like a baby and have been pain free ever since. In the twenty-four years of my Christian life I had been prayed for many times, but I had always woken up the next day back where I started—very sore and disappointed.

Secondly, and this is hard to put into words, my personality seems to have changed for the better—I'm more confident—especially at work. I used to feel quite immature and it bothered me. Now I really feel good about myself.

Thirdly, I am excited to say that I have not had to take the medication. I did not even have to wean myself off it gradually and I'm doing very well. I'm just in awe of how God works and how situations keep us in bondage and we can't get out of them by ourselves. God is truly amazing!

Jennifer's story is not unusual—forgiveness is a master key to healing in the very deepest recesses of our mind. What is unusual in Jennifer's story is that the person she most needed to forgive was herself.

Another lady had struggled with ME for seven years. Part of her ministry included forgiving herself for the ungodly sexual relationships of many years ago. She reported that, nearly a month later, she was still full of the joy of the Lord. Her back problem was healed, her relationships with others were changing and lots of fears had gone.

She was on a pilgrimage of healing and every day or two she noticed something was different. She summed it up this way, *"After twenty-eight years of Christian struggle the blockage between me and the Lord has been removed! I'm now enrolled in our church prayer ministry training course so I can learn how to help others experience this freedom too."*

Jan's Story

Jan was another lady for whom forgiving herself was the most important thing she had to do. Turning the master key of forgiveness for herself, proved to be the best thing she had ever done!

I gave my life to Christ twelve years ago. I raced right into ministry because Christ redeemed me and forgave me. I knew I was forgiven. I knew that He had washed me clean but I never forgave myself. I couldn't do that and I didn't know how. But I hit this wall and things got so hard.

I left home when I was seventeen. I made an awful lot of bad choices. I was so covered with the filth of shame in my life. I could say to people I want you so much to experience God's grace. But I was like a fake because I didn't own that for myself. I believed it but I didn't give myself permission to receive it by forgiving myself.

This weekend the labels that I have worn for forty-three years were ripped off. I am not ashamed any more. I am so thankful for that. Do you know what is like to feel rejected? On my rejection tree there was no room left since I filled so much of it up! I want to encourage all of you that He can give you what it takes to forgive yourself so that you can live in freedom for Him.

Michael's Story

Sometimes people come for prayer for something they know about, but God sees them as they really are and before long they are having to face the real issues. This was Michael's experience.

I arrived for the healing retreat expecting to deal with two traumatic accidents. But God had other ideas and I found myself having to deal with forgiveness in a mighty way! I also had to forgive myself for a lot of things and this was really liberating.

The Holy Spirit touched me deeply and filled me afresh. I am no longer in a spiritual wilderness. I have been so dry for the last few years and I had lost the joy of the Lord.

For the first time in my life (I'm fifty-four now) I feel as though I am truly "me." I have never understood why I used to say, "I wish I could just be me," but now I know! I have got rid of all the rubbish that was in my life and reclaimed my true self—as God created me to be. I now know who I am. Praise the Lord!

Connie's Story

Sometimes we find that people are damaged by circumstances that are beyond anyone's immediate control. There is nothing obvious that needs to be forgiven. But what I have seen on many occasions is that in circumstances like these there is a deep-down feeling that somehow or other it must be God's fault.

Part of the prayer ministry then has to include a prayer of saying sorry to God for blaming Him for things that have been a consequence of living in a fallen world, where Satan is ultimately behind everything that is bad. Connie's story falls into this category of deep inner pain. She truly experienced a miracle of God's grace as the earliest issues in her life were dealt with.

I went to a healing service not knowing what God needed to do, but I was open to Him. I went forward for prayer and as a result of this ministry both the cataracts in my eyes shrank—I was able to see shapes with my right eye, having been blind in that eye for ten years! I was also able to hear the ticking of the clock in my right ear—I had been unable to hear with that ear for ten years. I also had prayer about the severe curvature of my spine and this proved to be the start of the healing of my back condition.

My problems had begun in my mother's womb. I was born with brittle bones and at birth both my hips were dislocated. My mother was unable to show or express her love for me. She was afraid that in simply hugging me she would hurt my bones.

During the prayer ministry I found myself crying like a baby, and as the Holy Spirit moved upon me "chains" broke and something left my body. With that release came deliverance and I was set free from bondage. I saw Jesus, as if through a mist, wearing a white robe. He came, put His arms around me and said, "It's over, no more tears, you are saved. You are My child, My princess, and I have a special place for you."

My life has been changed—completely turned around. I'm walking daily with Him, experiencing the Holy Spirit strengthening me. He fills me with His joy and love and is continuing the healing in my body—my hips, head, eyes and ears, all of me. My confidence is back, I no longer need to use my white stick and can go out on my own. God has worked miracles and other people have seen the difference in me. I feel like my life has changed forever.

In praying for people like Connie we always pray to forgive anyone and everyone in the generational line who has done anything that has resulted in the condition she inherited. Sometimes that prayer alone begins a dramatic stage in the healing and restoration.

Olga's Story

Olga was brought up in communist Russia. Her parenting and ancestry left her very damaged emotionally, spiritually and even physically abused. The generational consequences of everything from occultism and witchcraft to the harshness of Russian communism had left its mark on Olga's life, resulting in a twisted spine and constant pain in her back, requiring regular treatment. It was seriously affecting her life. She had never linked her physical problems with the spiritual roots, but when she heard the message about how to forgive, she immediately knew what she had to do. God gave her the grace and here is her story of what happened.

I was brought up in Communist Russia. I always felt that I was under a generational curse because of my father's sincere embrace of communism and my grandmother's association with occult practices, even witchcraft, in pre-communist Russia. I didn't know my scoliosis of the spine and constant back pain was in any way connected to these things. But, but once I learned about the possible impact of such things I immediately recognized their relationship to my pain. At the conference I prayed deeply for freedom from generational sin and my mother's over-controlling spirit. I forgave from the deepest parts of my being and as I did so, I felt a ripple effect going down, and then up, my spine, as each vertebra responded to the movement of the Holy Spirit!

My back has been healed. Since then the pain from my childhood scoliosis has gone—every vertebra feels free of the tension from the past which interfered with my every movement. No more visits to the chiropractor since! No more fear of the past, or shadows waiting to catch me in my moment of doubt—they are powerless! They are gone—Hallelujah!

Bob's Story

Rejection comes in many forms. For Bob it was so deep it went to the very center of his being. His own Dad didn't want to know that this little boy was his. He was an embarrassment and his Dad did everything he could to disown the child that had been born to the woman he had a relationship with. But you cannot ever spiritually disconnect from those who are your children. No matter how or where they were conceived, they are always your children. Years later Bob just had to know what the truth really was. When his father was finally and positively identified, there began a new phase of his life trying to make it work. But the master key hadn't yet been turned in the lock of Bob's life. When it was, a miracle took place!

The most difficult issue in my life was the rejection that I felt from my earliest childhood, as the only son of a single mother. My father had, as a matter of legal strategy rather than real conviction, denied I was his son when I was very young. Even now I remember the cold December day when I took the blood test that established paternity. I spent a good part of my life trying to reconcile myself to my father after that—trying to be the 'good son' and make him (whether he liked it or not) the 'good father'.

While on a Healing Retreat at Ellel, and unbeknown to him, I asked God to break the ungodly soul-ties to my father as I forgave him. The result was an immediate and dramatically positive change in his life—a change that manifested itself at the very hour those ties were broken, even though he was 900 miles away! Suddenly he was liberated to be the 'good dad' he wanted to be, and I was liberated to love him in a godly way while building my relationship with my true Father in Heaven on solid spiritual ground. Now, my children enjoy their grandfather when he visits in ways that I could never enjoy him as a son. I love him with an unconditional love only Christ could have taught me to give. From Ellel's teaching I learned that there is no healing without forgiveness, and there is no forgiveness without genuine, Christ-like love. Like salvation itself, this is in fact a simple choice. Learn it for yourself, and be amazed, like I was, at what God can do!

In Conclusion

These stories are all real stories about real people. Real people like you and me who were struggling with the issues of life without realizing that the most important key to their problems lay in the area of forgiveness.

I pray that you will be encouraged to ask God to help you turn this master key and see His miracle-working power at work in your life as well.

For more information about the work of Ellel Ministries please see the website at www.ellelministries.org

Appendix

About Ellel Ministries

Our Vision

Ellel Ministries is a non-denominational Christian Mission Organization with a vision to resource and equip the Church by welcoming people, teaching them about the Kingdom of God and healing those in need (Luke 9:11).

Our Mission

Our mission is to fulfill the above vision throughout the world, as God opens the doors, in accordance with the Great Commission of Jesus and the calling of the Church to proclaim the Kingdom of God by preaching the good news, healing the broken-hearted and setting the captives free. We are, therefore, committed to evangelism, healing, deliverance, discipleship and training. The particular scriptures on which our mission is founded are Isaiah 61:1–7; Matthew 28:18–20; Luke 9:1–2; 9:11; Ephesians 4:12; 2 Timothy 2:2.

Our Basis of Faith

God is a Trinity. God the Father loves all people. God the Son, Jesus Christ, is Savior and Healer, Lord and King. God the Holy Spirit indwells Christians and imparts the dynamic power by which they are enabled to continue Christ's ministry. The Bible is the divinely inspired authority in matters of faith, doctrine and conduct, and is the basis for teaching.

Ellel Ministries Centers

International Headquarters

Ellel Grange
Ellel, Lancaster LA2 0HN, UK
t: +44 (0) 1524 751651 f: +44 (0) 1524 751738
e: info.grange@ellelministries.org

Ellel Glyndley Manor
Stone Cross, Pevensey, E. Sussex BN24 5BS, UK
t: +44 (0) 1323 440440 f: +44 (0) 1323 440877
e: info.glyndley@ellelministries.org

Ellel Pierrepont
Frensham, Farnham, Surrey GU10 3DL, UK
t: +44 (0) 1252 794060 f: +44 (0) 1252 794039
e: info.pierrepont@ellelministries.org

Ellel Scotland
Blairmore House, Glass, Huntly, Aberdeenshire AB54 4XH, Scotland
t: +44 (0) 1466 799102 f: +44 (0) 1466 700205
e: info.scotland@ellelministries.org

Ellel Ministries Northern Ireland
240 Rashee Road, Ballyclare, County Antrim, BT39 9JQ, Northern Ireland
t: +44 (0) 28 9334 4401
e: info.northernireland@ellelministries.org

Ellel Ministries Africa
PO Box 39569, Faerie Glen 0043, Pretoria, South Africa
t: +27 (0) 12 809 0031/1172 f: +27 12 809 1173
e: info.africa@ellelministries.org

Ellel Ministries Australia (Sydney)
Gilbulla, 710 Moreton Park Road, Menangle, 2568, NSW, Australia
t: +61 (02) 4633 8102 f: +61 (02) 4633 8201
e: info.gilbulla@ellelministries.org

Ellel Ministries Australia Headquarters (Perth)
Springhill, PO Box 609, Northam, WA, 6401, Australia
t: +61 (08) 9622 5568 f: +61 (08) 9622 5123
e: info.springhill@ellelministries.org

Ellel Ministries Canada
Derbyshire Downs
183 Hanna Rd., RR#2, Westport, Ontario, K0G 1X0, Canada
t: +1 (613) 273 8700
e: info.ontario@ellelministries.org

Ellel Ministries Canada West
10-5918 5 St SE, Calgary, Alberta, T2H 1L4, Canada
t: +1 (403) 238 2008 f: +1 (866) 246 5918
e: info.calgary@ellelministries.org

Ellel Ministries France
(Fraternité Chrétienne)
10 Avenue Jules Ferry, 38380 Saint Laurent du Pont, France
t: +33 (0)4 56 99 42 663
e: info.france@ellelministries.org

Ellel Ministries Germany
Bahnhoffstr. 43-47, 72213 Altensteig, Deutschland
w: http://www.ellelgermany.de
t: +49 (0) 7453 275 51
e: info.germany@ellelministries.org

Ellel Ministries Hungary
Veresegyház, PF17, 2112, Hungary
t/f: +36 28 362396
e: info.hungary@ellelministries.org

Ellel East Regional Nations
Veresegyház, PF17, 2112, Hungary
t: +36 28 362410 f: +36 28 362396
e: info.regionalnations@ellelministries.org

Ellel India
502, Orchid, Holy Cross Road, IC Colony, Borivli West, Mumbai 400 103, India
mobile: +91 (0) 93 2224 5209
e: info.india@ellelministries.org

Ellel Ministries Malaysia
Lot 2, Ground and 1st Floor, Wisma Leven Lorong Margosa 2, Luyang Phase 8, 88300
Kota Kinabalu, Sabah, Malaysia
t: +6088 270246 f: +6088 270280
e: info.malaysia@ellelministries.org

Ellel Ministries Netherlands
Wichmondseweg 19, 7223 LH Baak, Netherlands
t: +31 575 441452
e: info.netherlands@ellelministries.org

Ellel Ministries New Zealand
info.newzealand@ellelministries.org

Ellel Ministries Norway
Stiftelsen Ellel Ministries Norge, Hogstveien 2, 2006 Løvenstad, Norge (Norway)
t: +47 67413150
e: info.norway@ellelministries.org

Ellel Ministries Singapore
Thomson Post Office, PO Box 204, Singapore 915707
t: +65 6252 4234 f: +65 6252 3792
e: info.singapore@ellelministries.org

Ellel Ministries Sweden
Kvarnbackavägen 4 B, 711 92 Vedevåg, Sweden
t: +46 581 93140
e: info.sweden@ellelministries.org

Ellel Ministries USA
1708 English Acres Drive, Lithia, Florida, 33547, USA
t: +1 (813) 737 4848 f: +1 (813) 737 9051
e: info.usa@ellelministries.org

*All details are correct at time of going to press (September 2010) but are subject to change.

About the Author

Peter Horrobin is the Founder and International Director of Ellel Ministries. Ellel Ministries International was originally founded in 1986 as a ministry of healing in the northwest of England. The work is now (in 2008) established in about twenty different countries, and students who have trained with Ellel Ministries are working in every continent and in well over forty different countries.

Peter was born in 1943 in Bolton, Lancashire, England. His parents gave him a firm Christian foundation for life with a strong evangelical emphasis. His early grounding in the Scriptures was to equip him for future ministry.

After graduating from Oxford University with a degree in chemistry, he spent a number of years in college and university lecturing, before leaving the academic environment for the world of business.

He founded his own publishing and bookselling companies and then, after fifteen years of writing, publishing and bookselling, the doors opened for the ministry to be established at Ellel Grange, a country house just outside the city of Lancaster. Throughout his university and business career Peter had known that he was only "marking time" until his true calling, into some form of Christian ministry, would come to fruition.

Peter first knew this calling as a young teenager, but he had to wait nearly thirty years before his life's work was to begin! In his twenties he started to restore a vintage sports car (an Alvis Speed 20), but discovered that its chassis was bent. As he looked at the broken vehicle, wondering if it could ever be repaired, he sensed God asking him a question, *You could restore this broken car, but I can restore broken lives. Which is more important?*

It was obvious that broken lives were more important than broken cars, and so the beginnings of a vision for restoring people was birthed in his heart at that time. A few years later, he was asked to try and help a person who had been sexually abused. Through this experience God opened up to him the vision for the healing ministry. He prayed daily into this vision for over ten years before God brought it into being. Many Christian leaders affirmed the vision and gave it their support. Since then a hallmark of Peter's ministry has been his willingness to step out in faith and see God move to fulfill His promises, often in remarkable ways.

After the establishment of a Prayer Support Group, the purchase of Ellel Grange was completed in November 1986. Since then Ellel Ministries has grown very steadily—there is now a full-time team of over three hundred people, running a continuous series of healing retreats and training courses and schools at about twenty different centers around the world (See www.ellelministries.org for further information).

Peter is also an enthusiast of fishing and Alvis cars. His *Complete Catalogue of British Cars*, which was first published in 1975, has long been the standard reference work on the history and technical specification of every model of every make of British car manufactured between 1895 and 1975!

Peter and his wife, Fiona, live near Ellel Grange and now travel extensively to support and encourage the different Ellel teams. They have a particular responsibility within the ministry for pioneering new developments. Together they teach and minister on many different aspects of healing and discipleship.

For more information about Peter Horrobin, his career, ministry and publications please see www.ellelministries.org or go to his personal website at www.peterhorrobin.com.

Other titles in the Truth & Freedom Series

Also available in eBook format from all the major eBook retailers

Anger
How do you handle it?
Paul & Liz Griffin
RRP: £6.99
Size: 5.5"x8.5"
Pages: 112
ISBN: 9781852404505

Hope & Healing for the Abused
Paul & Liz Griffin
RRP: £7.99
Size: 5.5"x8.5"
Pages: 128
ISBN: 9781852404802

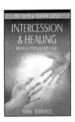

Intercession & Healing
Breaking through with God
Fiona Horrobin
RRP: £7.99
Size: 5.5"x8.5"
Pages: 176
ISBN: 9781852405007

Soul Ties
The unseen bond in relationships
David Cross
RRP: £7.99
Size: 5.5"x8.5"
Pages: 128
ISBN: 9781852404512

God's Covering
A place of healing
David Cross
RRP: £8.99
Size: 5.5"x8.5"
Pages: 192
ISBN: 9781852404857

The Dangers of Alternative Ways to Healing
How to avoid new age deceptions
David Cross & John Berry
RRP: £8.99
Size: 5.5"x8.5"
Pages: 176
ISBN: 9781852405373

Trapped by Control
How to find freedom
David Cross
RRP: £7.99
Size: 5.5"x8.5"
Pages: 112
ISBN: 9781852405014

Rescue from Rejection
Finding Security in God's Loving Acceptance
Denise Cross
RRP: £7.99
Size: 5.5"x8.5"
Pages: 160
ISBN: 9781852405380

Sex, God's Truth
Jill Southern
RRP: £7.99
Size: 5.5"x8.5"
Pages: 128
ISBN: 9781852404529

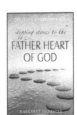

Stepping Stones to the Father Heart of God
Margaret Silvester
RRP: £8.99
Size: 5.5" x 8.5"
Pages: 176
ISBN: 9781852406233

www.sovereignworld.com

Other Products by Peter Horrobin

Healing through Deliverance (Hardback)

The Foundation & Practice of Deliverance Ministry

Peter Horrobin

Living the Life
Practical Christianity for the Real World

Peter Horrobin

The paperback book, 18-part DVD series (6 discs) and accompanying Study Guide. Ideal for home groups!

In this groundbreaking volume, Peter draws on his experience to set out a thorough scriptural foundation for the healing and deliverance ministry—an integral part of fulfilling the Great Commission and a vital key to discipleship.

He lays out the biblical basis for healing through deliverance; provides safe guidelines and practical tools for building a healing and deliverance ministry; helps people identify possible demonic entry points; and teaches how we can become affected by demonic power and how we can be delivered and healed.

A superb storyteller and seasoned teacher, Peter uses real life testimonies, parables and illustrations to unlock some of the most difficult theological and life issues that often make us stumble through our Christian walk.

What never seemed to make sense is suddenly crystal clear – even for the most experienced Christian. This book is an inspirational whistle-stop tour, flying through the galaxy of God's agenda, and bringing it back down to earth for all of us to discover how to live the life!

Related titles you may also be interested in...

Sarah
From an abusive childhood and the depths of suicidal despair to a life of hope and freedom

Sarah Shaw

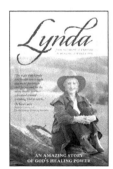

Lynda
From accident & trauma to healing & wholeness

Lynda Scott

www.sovereignworld.com

We hope you enjoyed reading this
Sovereign World book.
For more details of other
books and new releases see our website:

www.sovereignworld.com

Find us on:
Twitter @sovereignworld

Like us on:
www.facebook.com/sovereignworld

Our authors welcome your feedback on their books.
Please send your comments to our offices.
You can request to subscribe to
our email and mailing list online or by writing to:

Sovereign World Ltd, PO Box 784,
Ellel, Lancaster, LA1 9DA, United Kingdom
info@sovereignworld.com

Sovereign World titles are available from
all good Christian bookshops and eBook vendors.

For information about our distributors in the UK,
USA, Canada, South Africa, Australia and Singapore, visit:
www.sovereignworld.com/trade

If you would like to help us send a copy of this book and
many other titles to needy pastors in developing countries,
please write for further information or send your gift to:

Sovereign World Trust, PO Box 777,
Tonbridge, Kent TN11 0ZS
United Kingdom
www.sovereignworldtrust.org.uk

The Sovereign World Trust is a registered charity